Drop shipping:

A Step by Step Guide to Make Money Online and Create Passive Income with Dropshipping Using Advanced E-Commerce Business Model, Marketing Strategies, and Shopify Channel

Gabriele Undig

Table of Contents

Introduction

Chapter 1: Basics of Dropshipping and How it Works

   The Dropshipping Process

      Manufacturers

      Wholesalers

      Retailers

      Consumers

   How Does Dropshipping Work?

      Step 1: The Customer Places an Order with Your Online Store

      Step 2: You Place an Order with a Supplier Through Your Store

      Step 3: The Wholesaler/Supplier Ships the Order

      Step 4: You Send an Alert to the Customer of the Shipment

   Who Is Dropshipping for?

      First-Time Entrepreneur

      Budget Entrepreneur

      Validating Entrepreneur

Who Dropshipping Isn't for

  Margin-Focused Entrepreneur

  Brand-Centric Entrepreneur

  Non-Creative Marketer

Chapter 2: Achieve Financial Freedom with Dropshipping

Four Cs of Dropshipping

  Cost (What Is It That Makes Your Business Profitable?)

  Credibility (What Impact Does It Have on Your Brand?)

  Customer Service (What Impact Does Your Dropshipping Business Have on Your Customers?)

  Control (Who Has the Final Word on Customer Experience?)

Tips to Achieve Financial Freedom

  Recognize Where You Are

  Look at Money Positively

  Write Down Your Goals

  Track Your Spending

  Pay Yourself

  Spend Less

Pay Off Your Debt

Chapter 3: Advantages and Disadvantages of Starting a Dropshipping Business

Advantages of Dropshipping Business

It's Easy to Start

You Can Start with Low Investment

Low Overhead Costs

Easily Scalable

Wide Product Selection

Easy to Automate

Access to a Global Market

It's Easy to Find Manufacturers and Suppliers

Reduced Losses on Damaged Goods

More Time and Resources to Scale Your Business

You Can Run Your Business from Wherever You Are Located

Disadvantages of Dropshipping

Unrealistically Low-Profit Margins

Unexpected Stock Shortages

Lack of Full Control Over Customer Service

High Shipping Costs

Relying on the Availability of Stocks

You're Not Entirely in Control of the Business

Overcrowded Markets Make the Competition High

You Must Have Basic Technical Skills

You're Not Guaranteed Profits

Quality Control Issues

Working with More Products/Suppliers Means More Work

Errors by Suppliers

Complexities Associated with Shipping

Complete Liability in the Event of a Mishap

Difficulties Managing the Inventory

Chapter 4: How Dropshipping Can be a Successful Passive Income Business Model

Finding Suppliers

Contact the Manufacturer

Use Supplier Directories

Wholesale Central

Worldwide Brands

Identifying Fake Wholesalers

They Charge Ongoing Fees

  They Also Sell Products to the General Public

  They Don't Sign Any Contracts

Identifying Legitimate Wholesalers

  They Have a Minimum Size Order

  You Must Apply

  They Have Experienced Staff and a Dedicated Support Team

  They Have Pre-Order Fees

  Their Technology Isn't Up-to-Date

  They'll Not Persuade You to Work with Them

What You Need to Look for in a Supplier

  Their Location is Prime for Shipping

  They Take Orders by Mail

  They're Efficient in Order Processing

Before You Contact Suppliers

  Your Business Is Incorporated

  Know What You Want

  Ask If They Dropship

  Have Your Phone Ready

Paying Suppliers

PayPal

Credit Card

Net Terms

How to Deal with Suppliers

Get to Know Your Representative/Contact Person

Make Sure You Send Orders on Time

Dealing with Botched Orders

Apologize

Make It Up to the Customer

Let the supplier know about their mistake.

Chapter 5: What You Need to Start Your Dropshipping Business

The Power of Having the Right Mindset

Willingness to Act

Flexibility

Ability to Bounce Back

Things That You Need for Dropshipping

Value Proposition

Niche

The Right Product

Supplier

Registered Business

Strategy

Finances

Permits and Licenses

EIN Number

Sales Tax

Marketing Plan

Chapter 6: How to Choose the Best E-Commerce Solution

Things to Consider When Choosing an E-Commerce Platform

Payment and Pricing

Integrations

Customer Service

SEO Friendliness

Scalability

Security

E-Commerce Platforms to Consider

Amazon

Pros of Amazon Dropshipping

Cons of Amazon Dropshipping

eBay

Pros of eBay Dropshipping

Cons of eBay Dropshipping

Setting Up Your Own Website

Advantages of Setting up Your Own Dropshipping Website

Disadvantages of Setting Up your Own Dropshipping Website

Chapter 7: Niche Product or Not?

Identifying a Niche

Evergreen Niche Products

Evaluating Your Dropshipping Niche Ideas

Step 1: Find Trending or Niches with Low Competition

Is the Niche Product-Based?

The Popularity of the Niche

Check That the Niche Is Not Just a Passing Trend

How Passionate Are You About the Niche?

Will You Add Value to the Niche?

Step 2: Look Up Existing Retailers

Unsaturated or Saturated Niche?

Sustainability of the Niche

Closing a Sale

Chapter 8: Dropshipping Marketing Strategies to Increase Sales

Design a Terrific Interface for Your Store to Attract Customers

Social Media Integration

Email Marketing

Cross-Selling and Upselling Products

Engaging Customers via a Live Chat

Content Marketing

A Customer Loyalty Program

Dropship Private Label Products

How to Start Dropshipping Private Label Products

Checking Your Competition

Creating Your Customer Database

Chapter 9: How to Dropship on Shopify

Why Should You Start Dropshipping with Shopify?

Reasons Why Shopify Is Your Number One Pick for Financial Freedom

Visually Appealing

- *Easy to Set Up and Use*
- *Security and Reliability*
- *App Integration*
- *Powerful Marketing Tools*
- *Excellent Loading Speed*
- *Outstanding Customer Support*
- *Mobile Responsiveness*
- *Abandoned Cart Recovery*
- *Pricing and Affordability*
- *Easy Payment Gateway*

Using Shopify to Maximize the ROI
- *Name Your Dropshipping Store*
- *Create Your Shopify Account*
- *Optimize Your Shopify Account Settings*
- *Adding the Payment Information*
- *Adding Store Policies*
- *Shipping Rates*
- *Launching Your Shopify Dropshipping Store*
- *Designing Your Shopify Dropshipping Store*
- *Selecting A Theme for Your Shopify Dropshipping Store*

Creating A Logo

Add Your Products

Making Your First Sale

Optimizing Your Store for Selling

An Excellent Product Page

Product Description

A Clear Call to Action

Branding Your Dropshipping Store

Reliability

Authenticity

Conclusion

Introduction

Congratulations on downloading *Dropshipping*, and thank you for doing so!

Dropshipping is a business model with zero risks that lets you make passive income since you don't have to stock up any of the merchandise you're selling. Rather, you work closely with suppliers who drop ship products directly to your customers whenever a customer orders a product. While this may seem like a no-brainer, you need to be equipped with the relevant skills and knowledge before setting up your first dropshipping business.

This book offers answers to some of the questions that you may have and may be stopping you from taking action towards your first sale. *"What do I need to get started?" "How do you ensure your clients receive the product?" "What about guaranteeing customer satisfaction?"* Having all this information and more is the key to running a successful dropshipping business.

Dropshipping is your ultimate resource on how to make money through a dropshipping business. It's packed with all the information you need to start and successfully run your dropshipping business. In this book, I take you through the basics of dropshipping from understanding this business model to choosing a niche, making your first sale, and so much more.

Ultimately, you must be ready to put in hard work in order to begin seeing the results and making passive income. A positive attitude alone is not enough. You need to work on a number of things, including marketing, and this book helps you to master such skills. Moreover, get to know how to set up your dropshipping business with Shopify—a leading e-commerce platform for dropshipping.

There are plenty of books on this subject on the market—thanks again for choosing this one! Read on before beginning an exhilarating journey of making passive income with dropshipping. Every effort was made to ensure it is full of as much useful information as possible. Please enjoy!

Chapter 1: Basics of Dropshipping and How it Works

Dropshipping is a unique business model that allows you to sell products without necessarily having to own, buy, or even touch them. This means that you'll be an execution agent buying merchandise from a third party only when a customer makes a purchase from your online store. The product is usually shipped to the customer directly from the manufacturer or supplier. As a retailer, it is your sole responsibility to make sure that your client receives the product. This means that you're generating income, albeit in a passive way.

However, this isn't as simple as it may seem on paper, as it can be difficult to execute in reality. Thus, you have to invest in research, follow the right steps, and have the right intentions before you can begin to see the money. A basic principle in dropshipping that is critical to your success as a retailer is that you buy the product at a lower price and sell it at a higher price. What makes dropshipping an appealing way to do business is the fact that expenses are kept at a minimum while allowing you to set custom prices that allow you to make a reasonable profit. When you're equipped with the right information, you stand a better chance of running a successful dropshipping business.

Dropshipping is not an entirely new concept. Although the popularity of dropshipping has soared with access to the Internet, this model of doing business has been in existence long before there was the Internet. One of the motivating factors behind dropshipping is a quick turnaround that customers always appreciate. Before the internet age, retailers would employ this method of doing business to not only shorten the time it takes to get goods to their clients but also cut on the costs of getting them to the client. Therefore, instead of sending the inventory to the retailer who then sends the product to the customer, the wholesaler or manufacturer sends the merchandise directly to the customer. This was an excellent way of expediting delivery and ensuring customer satisfaction.

The digital age has perfected this business model, making it more accessible to many. The Internet has helped to cut through the barriers of time and space, making it possible for retailers to access international markets from the comfort of wherever they are. Dropshipping is a great opportunity, especially if you're savvy and are willing to go the long haul from research to actually set up your business. It entails selling products at their recommended retail value, collecting your payment from the customer, and then letting your supplier know that you need to ship a product to your customer. Are you wondering about how you get to make money? Well, it's simple. You'll buy the product at a wholesale price, so you have room to raise your preferred retail price as long as it's not exorbitant.

As a retailer, it's your duty to advertise, set up an e-commerce platform that is not just customer friendly but also secure and adhere to the government regulations relating to doing business. This includes the collection of the sales tax from customers and paying the state the taxes that you collect. What's even interesting is the fact that wholesalers have no limitation on the retailers; you can sell globally. The thing about dropshipping is that certain aspects of this model seem to be easy compared to others. However, in reality, your experiences and knowledge come in handy. Creating your e-commerce business thoughtfully by having a strong online presence lets customers come to purchase not only products but also receive items they purchase from your supplier or wholesaler.

The Dropshipping Process

It's important to have a good understanding of the dropshipping process before you set up your dropshipping business. To understand the process, you must know who the key players are and their role within the supply chain. In this context, a supply chain basically denotes the path a product follows from the time of development to production through to the customer who is also the user. There are a number of players involved along the supply chain as follows:

Manufacturers

This is basically the starting point of the supply chain because manufacturers or producers are involved in the creation of the product. However, in most instances, they don't sell these products to consumers but retailers and wholesalers. As a retailer, it's cheaper and more profitable to avoid middlemen and instead deal directly with the manufacturer. Even then, this is not always possible, especially if you're looking to start small because manufacturers have set a minimum number of purchases that might be out of reach for you. For instance, you might need just 100 pieces of a particular item, yet the manufacturer requires that you purchase at least 1,000 instead. In some instances, retailers may also stock products so that you ship them to customers whenever there's a purchase. This has made most retailers prefer working with wholesalers.

Wholesalers

Wholesalers are not involved in the production of goods. They only purchase goods in bulk for resale to retailers who in turn sell to consumers. Wholesalers make money by setting a markup on bulk orders from manufacturers to determine their profits. Generally, a wholesaler will have minimum purchase requirements than manufacturers. This is attributed to the fact that they are not involved in the production of goods; rather, they purchase various items and stock them in their warehouses. Moreover, you'll find that wholesalers deal in specified industries and niches. This means that while they may have a wide collection of products, these products belong to the same industry or niche. Like manufacturers, wholesalers don't sell to consumers directly; rather, they sell to retailers.

Retailers

This is where dropshippers fall. Retailers purchase goods from wholesalers, and in some instances, manufacturers to resell to consumers at markup price for profit. However, the difference lies in the fact that you're not directly involved in shipping the product to the customer. In most cases, shipping is the responsibility of the supplier. The interesting thing about this model is that all these players can take up the role of dropshippers. Even manufacturers can set up an in-house drop shipping operation center.

Consumers

Consumers are at the end of the chain/process. They're the ones who order and purchase goods for their own use, thus completing their fulfillment process. When a consumer receives a product, it signifies the process has been fulfilled, and the process is completed.

How Does Dropshipping Work?

With a proper perspective of the players involved in the dropshipping supply chain, you also need to understand the order process. Here's a step by step guide through the process:

Step 1: The Customer Places an Order with Your Online Store

The order is then approved, and a notification email is automatically generated by your store software and sent to both you and the customer. Payment from the customer is then captured when checking out, and the funds are automatically deposited to your store's bank account.

Step 2: You Place an Order with a Supplier Through Your Store

This is a simple step because all you need to do is forward the email order confirmations to your supplier's sales representative. Since the supplier already has your credit card on file, they will bill you for the goods at wholesale price. They will also include the processing and shipping fees.

Step 3: The Wholesaler/Supplier Ships the Order

Working with the assumption that the wholesaler has the product in stock and has successfully charged your account for the product, processing, and shipping of the product, the wholesaler will package the order and ship it to the customer. Although it's the wholesaler that is shipping the product, your business name, logo, and address will be provided on the address label as well as the packaging slip and the invoice. When the shipment is completed, the wholesaler sends you an email with the invoice and tracking number.

The turnaround time is usually faster than you'd imagine because some wholesalers ship out orders within a matter of hours, letting merchants advertise same-day shipping, which is one of the things customers look for when shopping.

Step 4: You Send an Alert to the Customer of the Shipment

Once you receive the tracking number, send it to the customer via the email that is built in your online store. With the order shipped, payment collected, and the customer notified of the same, the order and fulfillment process is finalized. Your profit is the difference between the money charged to the customer and what you paid to the wholesaler.

Who Is Dropshipping for?

Dropshipping is an incredible business model for anyone who wants to venture into online business for the first time. It's attractive to a rookie since there are low risk and low investment mode of starting a business without feeling like it's a huge gamble. Dropshipping is also ideal if you already have a store but are looking to expand your inventory by trying out specific products to gauge their performance before you stock up.

If you're considering dropshipping solely for the profit margins, then this is not a good idea. Instead, consider going to manufacturers. The challenge with manufacturers is that most of them will not facilitate dropshipping. Taking into account that the profit margins are considerably low compared to other models like wholesaling and manufacturing, dropshipping is not a good option for new start-ups because you don't have much control over customer satisfaction. Dropshipping will work well if you're:

First-Time Entrepreneur

Dropshipping is an excellent path to follow if you're venturing into online business for the first time. However, the truth is that doing business online is not a walk in the park. You have to spent and resources to drive traffic to your site and convert the traffic into sales. It'll take a while before you can figure this out. However, since you can begin your dropshipping business on a low budget, you can learn and act on the knowledge overtime to set up a vibrant store that will generate profit for you.

Budget Entrepreneur

Dropshipping is the least expensive mode of doing business since you don't have to invest in an inventory. As such, this method of doing business is ideal for entrepreneurs who are working on a budget and are keen on keeping the start-up costs as low as they can.

Validating Entrepreneur

Dropshipping can also work well if you're looking to test the perception and reception of new products in the market before you can invest in inventory. This makes it perfect if you need product validation before investing.

Who Dropshipping Isn't for

Based on the dynamics of the dropshipping business model, it isn't for everyone. You should avoid venturing into the dropshipping business if:

Margin-Focused Entrepreneur

One of the challenges of dropshipping is a thin margin. Usually, the gross margins for traditional drop shipping companies and products are between 10% and 20%. This goes even lower when you take into consideration other fees like shipping cart, transaction fees, email service as well as other app fees. This is a clear indication that dropshipping isn't a great choice if you're focused on margins.

Brand-Centric Entrepreneur

It can be incredibly difficult to attempt to build a sustainable brand through the dropshipping business model for the simple reason that you're not in control of the entire customer experience. There are times you'll have customers purchasing products that are sold out, leaving you frustrated, especially when you have to coordinate between your customer and the supplier, and this can leave a bad taste in the mouth of the customer.

Non-Creative Marketer

Don't make an attempt at dropshipping if you lack creativity when it comes to marketing. The reason for this is simple—it's likely that you're getting your products from the same suppliers as your competitors. This means that you're selling the same kind of products; hence, competing against them would mean that you employ a certain level of creativity and even find and exploit channels your competitors aren't using in order to acquire customers. Thus, this will not work if you lack creativity in the first place.

Just as it is with a traditional business, setting up a dropshipping business will require a certain level of effort, commitment, and passion for making it a success.

Chapter 2: Achieve Financial Freedom with Dropshipping

Financial freedom often sounds like a theory. However, it's possible for anyone to achieve financial freedom with dropshipping no matter the kind of troubles you may be facing today. But just what is financial freedom? In simple terms, financial freedom is all about taking ownership of your finances such that you have a cash flow that is dependable and lets you live the kind of life that you want. This means that you will not be worrying about how you'll pay your bills or even sudden expenses. And most importantly, you're not burdened by debt—that is, financial freedom lets you recognize that you are able to pay your own debt while also increasing your income with a side hustle. Most importantly, it's about planning your long term financial situation by saving actively for the rainy day.

One of the decisions that you will make about dropshipping could also usher you into financial freedom. This means that you must make a critical decision on how you'll not only control but also distribute the products that you will sell through your dropshipping store. This chapter examines ways through which you can achieve financial freedom with dropshipping.

Four Cs of Dropshipping

Generally, for you to manage a profitable e-commerce business, you need to have resilience, a strategy, and, of course, a bit of trial and error. Remember, the logistics of running your business could change drastically through time. It's never the same every day. This means that you must be ready and willing to make changes, no matter how scary it is. However, you must take caution so that you don't immerse yourself fully into dropshipping before you familiarize yourself with what it is that you're getting yourself into. A good place to start your journey to financial freedom is finding the right suppliers/manufacturers. You also have to consider the following four Cs:

Cost (What Is It That Makes Your Business Profitable?)

When you talk about cost, you need to consider the cost of handling your inventory against the cost of outsourcing the same responsibility to a wholesaler. Although drop shipping is great in terms of the ease of deploying and arranging, it can eat into your profits when you don't do your homework well and offset the costs. This means that you have to look into the kind of distribution model that will support your long term profit margin. It could mean looking into specific suppliers and the fees they charge. It could be probable that you can increase the profit margins of your business by opting to go for a mixture of fulfillment methods. There's no reason that can stop you from adopting dropshipping for larger orders while keeping the smaller as well as bespoke orders for internal handling and processing. You could have big clients who want to deal directly with you and give you more quality control over the client service. This is okay if it'll make your business more sustainable. Using an out-of-the-box platform like Shopify makes it easy to upload products and get started with sales, albeit with minimum commitment. Such platforms offer a plethora of information together with a hub of experienced business owners who are talking about the same issues you may be facing and sharing all the valuable lessons. Although dropshipping through out-of-the-box platforms works well, allowing your business to generate income on a huge investment because you may want to have a custom website in the case where you're responsible for shipping the products. Thus, you have to weigh what is important to the business and your audience against the cost of setting up and maintenance. Always keep in mind that cost is not just short term viability of your business and making an initial margin. You always have to look at the bigger picture to factor in where you're going to operate from, the cost of working on a large site, and the cost of scaling up your business, among other things.

Credibility (What Impact Does It Have on Your Brand?)

You need to ask yourself if you're able to vouch for products you're selling when you haven't seen them. Are you certain about the quality and can guarantee your customers the same? Well, to achieve financial freedom with dropshipping, you must make sure that your efforts are all geared towards building brand credibility and reputation. This can then help you to justify the cost of the inventory or even shipping. The reason for this is simple—when you're comfortable about your credibility to customers, you can be sure to make sales even when you're not doing aggressive marketing campaigns. This can usher you into incredible financial freedom even as you focus on improving the areas where you need to reinvest.

Customer Service (What Impact Does Your Dropshipping Business Have on Your Customers?)

It's almost impossible to be in complete control of your customer satisfaction for your dropshipping business, yet customer service is the heart of attaining financial freedom. However, you can take a different approach where you keep your customers in the loop of all the development from the time of purchase to the time they receive their parcel. This includes bringing them up to speed on delays as well as thanking them for making the purchase. You can also have a simple return process so as to ensure that customer issues are addressed exhaustively.

Control (Who Has the Final Word on Customer Experience?)

You must ask yourself if you're able to take full control of the purchase and sale processes while managing complaints that may arise sufficiently. How are you controlling the revenue flow, and how does this impact your startup costs? For you to achieve true financial freedom, you must be able to control your business, particularly paying attention to the cash flow. You'll need to use accounting software that has been designed to help you manage your sales and inventory on multiple channels in addition to managing canceled orders and returns. Invest in a system that allows you to streamline processes.

Tips to Achieve Financial Freedom

Here are some tips to help you achieve financial freedom with dropshipping:

Recognize Where You Are

It's almost impossible to attain financial freedom with dropshipping when you don't even know your starting point.

You first need to recognize where you are. Establish how much debt you have versus your savings, as well as how much money you require. This can be a difficult reality to handle but a step in the right direction. Come up with a list of your debts, which could be anything from student loans, mortgage, credit cards, car loans, or any other debt that you have accumulated. Make sure you include all the money you may have borrowed from family and friends over time. Don't freak out if your debt is too big. You'll be surprised that you can settle all these debts over time. If your debt is small, the better. In the same manner, take stock of your savings and keep these numbers in mind as you work through the next steps.

Look at Money Positively

Having huge debts to pay off can be discouraging when you're beginning your dropshipping store. However, you must constantly keep in mind that money is a good thing. For you to experience financial freedom, you will need to view money as a tool to help you fuel your energy, achieve your dreams, and live a stress-free life you can enjoy. Viewing money negatively will sabotage your chances subconsciously.

Write Down Your Goals

It's likely that you are looking to start your dropshipping business to make money and attain financial freedom. But there's more to just making money. It could be that you also want to get out of debt or better still an escape from the 9 to 5 grind. Or you simply want to travel to the world. When you tie these goals to your dropshipping business, you will have the motivation to work towards making more money so that you see your debts diminish as your savings increase. Seeing the numbers change is a great motivation towards achieving your goals. Even then, you must approach it with the realization that you're not able to accomplish everything

Track Your Spending

This is an important step to financial freedom. When you are able to keep track of your expenditure, you'll be able to tell how much money you're spending and the areas you're spending on. Similarly, you will be able to know your income and tell whether your goals are realistic or not. You can use an app to help you stay focused on your financial goals.

Pay Yourself

This principle has helped many people to achieve financial freedom. Paying yourself means you have control over your income and have a better chance of saving because you'll always set aside some money to save as well as invest in yourself. When you don't pay yourself, you'll not have a substantial amount of money to experience financial freedom.

Spend Less

Frugality is the reason why some people have achieved financial freedom. Don't spend more than you need to or even what you don't have. You don't have to look like a rich person. Instead, train yourself on nurturing your dropshipping business so that your income flow is steady. When you spend less, you'll have more to spare, so you'll be putting aside more money.

Pay Off Your Debt

You may want to invest your money first before paying off debt. However, the truth is that when you pay debt first, it gives you a chance to save and invest your money elsewhere, which brings you closer to financial freedom. Paying off debt takes off weight from your shoulders because you will now begin to see the money you have in the bank increasing.

Dropshipping can help you take charge of your finances when you approach it with a good strategy. When you follow the financial freedom tips discussed above, you'll sure get closer to achieving the financial freedom that seems elusive.

Chapter 3: Advantages and Disadvantages of Starting a Dropshipping Business

Advantages of Dropshipping Business

One of the reasons why dropshipping continues to attract people who are keen to generate passive income is because it offers so many advantages. Here are some of the advantages of dropshipping:

It's Easy to Start

You'll be surprised to know that you can actually start your dropshipping business wherever you are in just under an hour. All you'll need is the product, a website, access to the relevant tools, software, and plugins that are designed to facilitate the dropshipping process. With these tools in hand, you can be sure of starting and running your business fast. Furthermore, some of these tools also help you to automate the business to you don't have to dedicate all your time to your business. Now, you're probably wondering how to create your website when you don't have the technical expertise of a web designer. You can create your own site by taking advantage of the tons of templates that are suitable for dropshipping. All you have to do is customize your template to suit your needs then upload the products you're selling or promoting. Building your website is generally easy, especially when you already know the products you will be selling and their feature as these determine the kind of content you will publish.

You Can Start with Low Investment

You don't need so much money to start your dropshipping business for the simple reason that you're not holding an inventory. Instead, you only purchase from a product from a manufacturer or supplier when a customer places an order through your website. Even then, this cost doesn't mean much because you'll still get profit from the sale. The actual you need to consider in order to set up your dropshipping business includes costs relating to setting up the website such as web development, domain registration and hosting, website maintenance, and advertising. Although you can find some of them for free, you could also pay for plugins, add-ons, software programs, and other tools you'll need for the smooth running of your dropshipping website. While some of these may attract a recurring fee like a monthly subscription, others only require a one-time fee. Costs relating to the inventory will often depend on the nature of deals and negotiations you hold with the manufacturer and supplier. Even then, these costs can't compare to the traditional model of doing business.

Low Overhead Costs

Overhead costs are usually a big problem for most traditional businesses. The good news is that with dropshipping, you're not keeping an inventory, so you're unlikely to have overhead costs. Some of the overhead costs that dropshipping does take off include interest on bank loans towards the purchase of inventory, warehousing/storage racks, as well as the cost of obsolescence where the inventory item ends up not being used either because the technology is outdated or due to perishability. Even better, your overhead costs go down with time since a big part of the overhead costs will be in the initial stages before they begin decreasing with time. The reason for this is simple. You're likely to make mistakes that will expose you to certain risks. However, as you get better, you'll be making strategic moves, thus minimizing overhead expenses.

Easily Scalable

The dropshipping model of doing business makes it easy to scale up. The growth of a brick and mortar business means expanding space, growing your staff as well as your inventory. The dropshipping model is quite different because as your business grows, it is your suppliers or manufacturers who have to handle the bulk of work while you handle the traffic. This means you have ample time to take care of what needs your attention, such as customer service or growing your inventory. You can even opt to create another dropshipping website altogether because there's no limit to the number of websites you can create as long as you're able to manage them, especially if you have the relevant tools and can master automation.

Wide Product Selection

It's widely assumed that you can only sell up to two products with dropshipping. This is not true. Owing to the nature of dropshipping that doesn't require you to have to keep in inventory, you have the freedom to sell more than one product without any risks. The most important thing is to make sure that your customers receive the product. You can liberally choose to sell hundreds or dozens of products from the thousands of products that are available for sale via dropshipping. Even then, the challenge is how to manage the orders of varying products without being overwhelmed or leaving out some customer orders, as this will definitely compromise customer satisfaction. For this reason, it's advisable that you begin with one product and gradually scale up so once you're comfortable with running your business. The rule of thumb is that don't go for more than you can handle.

Easy to Automate

Doing business online makes it easy to get a couple of things done by simply automating processes. For instance, you can set up your website with a few clicks. Once your site is up and running, you can use the relevant plugin to execute certain functions. For instance, you can have a "chatbot" running on artificial intelligence to take care of your customer service features. Automation is an excellent way of freeing up time as well as letting the business run smoothly with minimal intervention hence letting you earn passive income. With automation, you can be sure of making sales at any time of day or night, and even when you are on vacation! You just need to check occasionally to be sure that there are no errors or bugs in the system so that you dedicate your time to marketing and driving traffic to your site.

Access to a Global Market

The beauty of dropshipping is that the market does not limit you. You're free to sell locally or internationally as long as manufacturers or suppliers are able to ship the product yours to customers. Dropshipping doesn't have the limitation of location because you just need a simple website to reach out to millions of potential customers globally. Even then, you must be able to factor in the costs associated with shipping products to different countries as these often vary and can be too expensive in some instances that will eventually cost you money. Alternatively, aim at pricing your products based on the buyer's geographical location. This way, the price will be realistic because it's determined by taking in the shipping costs within that particular country into consideration. This means that you build a dynamic website so that customers can see different prices based on their location.

It's Easy to Find Manufacturers and Suppliers

There are hundreds of thousands of manufacturers and suppliers who are already working with retailers to fulfill their orders.

Reduced Losses on Damaged Goods

Because the products are shipped directly from the supplier to your customer and you are not involved in the shipment steps, there are minimal chances of risk of having to deal with damaged items when moving from one location to the other.

More Time and Resources to Scale Your Business

Unlike the traditional model of doing business where you have to do more work and invest more resources in realizing profits, dropshipping lets you handle very little percent of the process, so you're left with ample time to develop and scale your business.

You Can Run Your Business from Wherever You Are Located

You don't need a warehouse to an office or even employees to start a dropshipping business. Dropshipping is location independent, and with little or no commitment to physical space, you can run your business from anywhere and still manage to make your profit. All you need is your laptop, digital tools, and a good Internet connection.

Disadvantages of Dropshipping

It'll be naïve to assume that with all the advantages discussed above, dropshipping doesn't have any disadvantages. The truth is that dropshipping has its own shortcomings that you need to know so that you're well prepared to handle them if and when they arise. Here are some drawbacks of this model of doing business:

Unrealistically Low-Profit Margins

Although you're sourcing your goods from manufacturers and suppliers at a fairly "good" price, the truth is that the price is usually higher compared to the price a stocking retailer will pay. That is a retailer operating a brick and mortar store and keeps an inventory. This is attributed to a number of factors that include overhead costs, among other factors. It's important that you weigh in on this price difference, especially if the products your selling are readily available in most of the retail outlets. The reason for this is simple—if the cost of goods is higher, chances are your prices will be higher in comparison to the other retailers, and this is likely to work against you because your profit margins may end up being ridiculously low.

Unexpected Stock Shortages

This is a common challenge that most entrepreneurs who are engaging in dropshipping do experience, yet you have very little control over. This may be due to a surge in orders for certain products that the supplier cannot handle, yet they are dealing with different other dropshippers. In most cases, stock shortages are a result of inconsistencies in the many in which orders from customers are coming in. To be on the safe side, you can leverage online tools to analyze trends in relation to the seasonality of the products you're selling. This way, you can be able to anticipate seasons of high demand—for instance, during holidays or the festive season. This way, you can also link up with more suppliers so that you're able to meet the needs of your customers comfortably.

Lack of Full Control Over Customer Service

While it's the supplier who does the shipping of products to your customers, you are responsible for the quality of customer service. This is obviously a problem because you are not in control of the packaging and shipping; hence, you're not in the loop about when and how the products get to your customers. In cases where your customers are disgruntled, you have to follow up on so many factors on the shipping process that include the shipping date, tracking details, as well as the estimated time of arrival, among other things. Only then can you be able to provide an appropriate response or solution that may include a refund.

High Shipping Costs

One thing you need to know is that although it's the manufacturer of supplier that ships the product to your customer, you actually pay for the shipping. Therefore, you not only pay for the product but also the pay for other related costs relating to stocking, packaging, and ultimately shipping. This definitely marks a significant difference in the actual profit that you can make from a sale. As such, you need to be very good at negotiating with the manufacturer and supplier so that they give you a fairer rate that will not push the fulfillment costs up.

Relying on the Availability of Stocks

Since you don't get to keep an inventory, your business is at the mercy of the manufacturer or supplier. It means that you're operating on the goodwill that they will always have stocks. In the worst-case scenario, if a supplier is always telling you the stocks are not available every so often, you could as well close your store because if you don't, you end up with a bad reputation that isn't good for business. You may want to deal with reliable suppliers or have a network of suppliers, so if one fails, you can count on the other.

You're Not Entirely in Control of the Business

It's unfortunate that most people ignore this fact only to have to deal with it later. The fact that you're relying on a third party to fulfill your customer orders means that you don't have control over your business. If anything, the shipping process is quite risky because it can be marred by delays, damage, or even loss of items, and the customer will lay the blame squarely on you and not the supplier. In fact, the customer doesn't even recognize the manufacturer or the supplier but you; thus, it's your brand that will suffer.

Overcrowded Markets Make the Competition High

So many people have embraced the dropshipping model that is has gone mainstream. Consequently, there's stiff competition among sellers, with most of the markets being too crowded already. In fact, this can only get worse in the future as more late bloomers attempt to embrace the trend. This means that as you set up your dropshipping business, you must be ready to compete with existing and new sellers so that your business stands out. This could mean investing in research or niching down so that you only deal with those products that have good demand but are not as competitive.

You Must Have Basic Technical Skills

Unknown to many people, you require technical skills to run a successful dropshipping business. The reason is simple. Most of the things you need involve either building or managing your website. Therefore, it's only reasonable when you have some basic technical skills. Although you may want to consider getting an expert to set up and manage your website, this may be costly in the long run. Moreover, having technical know-how means you can comfortably fix any technical problems that may arise to ensure the smooth running of your website. This means that you don't have to wait for too long if customers are unable to place an order, the site is taking too long to load, or there's an issue with payment processing, among other things.

You're Not Guaranteed Profits

A common misconception most people hold is that it's easy to make a profit with dropshipping since you don't hold any inventory and have minimal overhead costs. They assume that you make huge profits from a single sale because it is the supplier that ships the products to your customers. In reality, there's no guarantee about making a profit with dropshipping just as it is with any other business. A number of things could go wrong, such as losing a deal with your supplier, the goods delivered could be subpar, overestimating the market potential, or not being able to sell at all. If any of these happens, it's unlikely that you'll make any profit. In fact, you could end up losing some money.

Quality Control Issues

The fact that you're not in control of product development, manufacturing, and handling, you don't have much control over the quality. While you need to agree with the supplier on the quality issues to ensure that the standards are not compromised, you don't have a guarantee that the quality will always meet your standards. You just have to assume that your supplier will meet their end of the deal. You can only rely on the feedback from your customers in case the quality of products is compromised. Unfortunately, this may be a little too late because you'll have to work on rebuilding a positive relationship with your customers.

Working with More Products/Suppliers Means More Work

Although it's easy to scale up your dropshipping business, you need to know that adding more products and suppliers translates to more work for you. This is something you can easily overlook because you're eager to increase your earnings. However, you must be aware of the fact that this will not come easy. It could actually get complicated when you have to deal with multiple suppliers to fulfill one customer's order. Besides, managing and tracking different suppliers and orders can be a huge challenge. Ultimately, you'll do well to evaluate your capacity before scaling up and bringing more suppliers on board so that you only take on what you can handle comfortably.

Errors by Suppliers

Don't expect your supplier to be perfect. In fact, no manufacturer or supplier is perfect. They all are bound to make errors when processing your customer orders. This may be anything from sending the wrong product to the right customer or vice versa. It's a common occurrence to have products with wrong specifications being sent to customers, and it can be very frustrating because you really don't have much control over such errors. Should you receive customer complaints on such errors, you must work to make sure that the wrong product is recalled and the right product is resent.

Complexities Associated with Shipping

Shipping products to clients is not an easy endeavor even though it is the responsibility of the manufacturer or supplier. You need to ensure that there's a smooth connection between the sale process and the shipping process. This way, the supplier receives an invitation immediately a customer places their order. The sooner the supplier receives information about the sale, the faster they're able to affect the shipping. Lack of efficient communication between your business and the supplier or manufacturer could result in complexities that can ruin your business.

Complete Liability in the Event of a Mishap

The customer doesn't know about the suppliers and their role in your business. They only recognize you, the retailer. Therefore, if something goes wrong or the supplier messes something, it is your fault because your brand is the face of the business. This is why you must make sure you find a good supplier.

Difficulties Managing the Inventory

It's impossible to monitor your supplier's stock. An error in communication could necessitate the cancellation or placing orders on the backorder. While this can be managed digitally, it comes at an additional cost that could increase your fixed costs as well as overhead costs.

Chapter 4: How Dropshipping Can be a Successful Passive Income Business Model

Now that you understand what role you'll be playing in the dropshipping chain, you now need to work on building relationships with the other players who are equally important. That is, the suppliers. This chapter takes you through ways of finding and contacting suppliers. I will also highlight some of the pitfalls you're likely to make as a first time dropshipper when looking for suppliers.

Finding Suppliers

The process of finding suppliers should be straightforward. After all, you're bringing business right at their doorstep. Who wouldn't want that? Well, that is what most dropshippers assume. In reality, you need to approach the process of finding a supplier with tact and caution. You must use the right strategies to be able to single out good suppliers from bad ones. Ultimately, you need to find suppliers who are reliable. Here are some strategies to get you started:

Contact the Manufacturer

This is often seen as the easiest method of finding a wholesaler. When you have figured out the kind of goods you want to sell, find out about who makes those products and get in touch with them. You can then request them to share with you the list of their wholesalers so that you're working with an official list provided by the manufacturer. This gives the assurance that you're working with businesses that are legitimate.

The good thing about using this strategy is that it's fast, and you can execute it with a few calls. You simply need to place a few calls to different manufacturers in the niche you've selected. Don't be surprised if you find the names of some suppliers recurring from one manufacturer's list to the other. In fact, this is always an indication of who the leading wholesalers are.

Use Supplier Directories

Although suppliers will not charge you connection fees, using a supplier directory will require you to pay a monthly charge. Generally, a supplier directory will list wholesalers in just about every niche. Using directories guarantees you security while at the same time offering convenience. Directories are usually secure since they must screen wholesalers before they can list them. They also bring inconvenience because they give you a chance to look at wholesalers either by product or by niche. This can save you a lot of time, especially when you have to look for so many suppliers.

Supplier directories are a great place to start if you have some money you can spend on them. However, you also need to know that it's possible to find the wholesalers even without using the directory. If you can find suppliers on your own, then you don't really need the directory. Even then, keep in mind that using a directory will save you time and usher you to a world of suppliers. Some of the leading supplier directories are:

Wholesale Central

The fact that this directory is free serves as a red flag. This directory has a number of issues. While suppliers are charged for the listing, not all the suppliers who are listed are genuine. In fact, the majority of the wholesalers listed here are retailers who are selling products at wholesale price. While the directory managers claim to screen the applicants, they are not specific on what the screening process entails. This makes it possible that illegitimate suppliers are making their way through it.

Worldwide Brands

This is among the oldest directories that are most trustworthy. This directory boasts of a huge database of certified wholesalers. The wholesalers are all top-level; thus, there are no middlemen. Moreover, you can also be sure to find millions of products in this directory. To access this directory, you'll be required to pay a lifetime membership of $299 that is a great deal compared to many directories you will find. If you intend to use a directory to find the best suppliers, then Worldwide Brands is a good choice.

Identifying Fake Wholesalers

The dropshipping business is not risk-free. You may come across fake wholesalers who are after your money but are not ready to deliver products to your customers. This means you need to know how to identify fake wholesalers so that you are well protected from fraudsters. Some retailers will pose like wholesale suppliers to increase their sales. However, they mark up their prices like crazy—meaning that you'll have a slight margin. You need to work with wholesalers who are buying directly from the manufacturer because they will offer you better pricing.

It's not that easy to tell a fake wholesaler apart from a genuine one. It's actually almost impossible. The reason is that fake wholesalers appear to be credible. This is worsened by the fact the legitimate wholesalers are usually less marketing savvy making it quite difficult to find them. Unfortunately, fake marketers often put up a vibrant marketing campaign so that they are visible with just about every search.

Here are three things to help you spot fake wholesalers:

They Charge Ongoing Fees

This is one of the ways fake suppliers milk money from unsuspecting dropshippers. They charge you a monthly fee for doing business with them. This is not sensible and genuine wholesalers would never do this. However, you should not confuse this with wholesaler directories that charge a fee. In fact, directories are a good way of getting suppliers.

They Also Sell Products to the General Public

Most of the retailers who pose as wholesalers will also be selling to the general public where they advertise wholesale prices. This is a trick to make customers believe they're getting a good deal. However, in reality, they inflate prices when adding the wholesale label. This is a sign that they are actually fake. Real wholesalers will not sell goods to the public. Besides, you usually have to apply to make a deal with a wholesaler and wait to be approved because you also have to prove your own business is legitimate.

They Don't Sign Any Contracts

This is another red flag that will enable you to identify fake wholesalers. When getting into an agreement with a wholesaler, it's always important that you sign a contract that is legally binding. However, fake suppliers will refuse to sign any contract and dismiss it as being unnecessary.

Identifying Legitimate Wholesalers

Knowing how to identify a fake wholesaler is not enough. It's equally important to know how to find a legitimate wholesaler you can work with for your dropshipping success. You can use the following criteria to find real wholesalers:

They Have a Minimum Size Order

It's a common thing to find that wholesalers have set a minimum order size, particularly for your first order. This is because suppliers want to work with serious businesses only. Thus, setting a minimum order will filter those people who are not serious but are only window shopping. Even then, in some cases, the minimum order can be a challenge for some dropshippers, especially those who can't seem to meet the minimum order. To address this, you can always talk to the supplier to convert the difference to credit that can be applied to future orders.

You Must Apply

While fake wholesalers don't require you apply to be approved to do business with them, legitimate wholesalers have made this a mandatory requirement that you must meet. This means that your company must be legally incorporated, and the supplier must approve of you. This must happen before you can access the suppliers' price list.

They Have Experienced Staff and a Dedicated Support Team

This is the guarantee of a leading supplier. You should be able to call a representative that not only understands your niche but can also respond to any questions that you may have in detail. If you find company representatives that are known to be knowledgeable, the chances are that they do not have prior training or experience. You must also search for a dedicated support team. Most wholesalers will assign you to a specific customer support member to handle all your queries and needs. This eliminates the confusion that comes with having to call multiple members of the team.

They Have Pre-Order Fees

Although you're not required to pay a monthly fee, some wholesalers will charge pre-order fees. This can range from $1 to $5 for each order. This could actually go up depending on the size of the order.

Their Technology Isn't Up-to-Date

Legitimate wholesalers are not only poor at marketing. They also tend to be poor with technology. While this is not a deal-breaker, it's always good to work with a wholesaler with a polished website and interface where you can look at certain features like a real-time inventory, a searchable order history, and easy to use online catalogs as these save you time.

They'll Not Persuade You to Work with Them

In most cases, middlemen will strive to persuade you to work with them because they're simply retailers. However, this is very different from wholesalers as they will only provide you the relevant information and leave you to make a decision on whether you'll work with them or not.

What You Need to Look for in a Supplier

The fact that a supplier is legitimate alone is not a reason enough to make them the best option. In reality, choosing the right supplier is a lengthy process. However, it's quite fulfilling when you finally find one that meets all your criteria. If you're just getting into dropshipping, you probably don't have an idea about where to begin your search for suppliers. Here are some pointers to help you find the right supplier:

Their Location is Prime for Shipping

Always think about the suitability and convenience of the supplier's location in relation to the ease of shipping. It makes sense to go for a supplier who is in a prime location that makes it possible to have customer orders shipped within the shortest time possible. A supplier who is in a central location will give you consistent shipping results. In most cases, you'll have customers receiving their packages within a few days.

They Take Orders by Mail

Although having to call for an order may not seem like a big deal, in the beginning, it's definitely the best way to go when you begin getting too many orders in a single day. It'll definitely be more hectic to call in to place orders compared to simply placing your orders via email.

They're Efficient in Order Processing

You definitely don't want to work with a supplier who will botch orders or make mistakes that will be costly for your dropshipping business. You must make sure that you settle for a supplier that will handle your orders efficiently. You can begin by placing test orders to see how the supplier will handle them from your side. If the supplier fails to furnish you with the tracking information on time, that could be a red flag. Make sure the entire process is smooth and seamless.

Before You Contact Suppliers

Once you have identified suppliers that you could work with, you must take care of a number of things before you can reach out to them. They include the following:

Your Business Is Incorporated

There is no compromise about this. The majority of wholesalers will want proof to show that your business is incorporated. Most of them will only show you their pricing once you meet this requirement.

Know What You Want

It's important that you clearly define what it is that you want from the dropshipper. Make sure you have all the specifics in mind before making that contact them. The reason for this is simple. By now, you know wholesalers are busy, yet they get tons of spam daily, so you don't want to be classified among those. Just get straight to the point, and the supplier will tell that you're serious.

Ask If They Dropship

It's wrong to make an assumption that the supplier does dropshipping because it'll be quite inconveniencing to find out that they don't dropship later when you probably have an order. Moreover, it'll also save you time so that you don't spend too much time engaging them with questions only to learn they can't dropship.

Have Your Phone Ready

As a dropshipper, you don't have to do everything on your computer. Instead, you can invest in a good phone that you'll be using to shoot emails conveniently from wherever you are.

Paying Suppliers

Once you've found a good supplier and have sealed a deal, you need to find out how you will pay the suppliers so that there are no hitches when you need to pay. Some of the common payment options include the following:

PayPal

Although not all suppliers will receive payment via PayPal, many do because it's universal. Moreover, it's a convenient way of paying even though it involves transaction fees, which is one of the reasons that some suppliers shun from using it.

Credit Card

This is the most preferred mode of payment because almost all suppliers accept payment via credit card. It's convenient, fast, and secure. Moreover, it doesn't attract transactional charges like PayPal, which is one of the reasons why it's most preferred.

Net Terms

This is a traditional method where you pay for products you have purchased after a certain number of days. While there's a risk of customers getting away with supplier's money, this is catered for by suppliers requiring that you give them credit references.

How to Deal with Suppliers

Have you stopped to think about your responsibilities when dealing with the supplier? Here are some general rules that can guide you when handling suppliers:

Get to Know Your Representative/Contact Person

A good supplier should assign you a representative that is dedicated to handling your issues. This means you have to build a good rapport with your representative because you will be talking to them whenever you have any issues with your order. In case you experience any issues with the representative, make sure you talk about it because a bad representative could be the reason for all your orders going wrong.

Make Sure You Send Orders on Time

You must send the orders to the supplier on time for them to execute your order on time. The supplier needs to get your customer's order in a speedy manner, and this is all dependent on how soon you notify them.

Dealing with Botched Orders

Dropshipping has its own share of challenges, among them botched orders. Suppliers can mess up an order, particularly if they are always getting a high volume of orders. Botched orders can be anything from sending the wrong item to the right customer or failing to ship the item. Whatever the case, you need to know how to remedy the mistake. Here's a three-step process to correct the mistake:

Apologize

You must first admit the mistake and apologize to the customer. This is not the time to start blaming the supplier, as this will only taint your reputation as a retailer. If anything, the supplier doesn't need to know about the supplier.

Make It Up to the Customer

An apology alone is not enough. You need to correct the mistake. This may require that you send the right product or issues a refund of the shipping cost or even send the customer a freebie. Whatever it is you need to do, make sure you make things right.

Let the supplier know about their mistake.

Once you have settled the issue with the customer, you can go ahead and let the supplier know about their mistake and possibly pay for it. This would mean that the supplier covers the shipping cost for resending the right item or the cost of returning the wrong item.

Ultimately, you need to monitor the manner in which your supplier handles orders so that you are able to flag down a rogue supplier before the damage gets out of control. While it's true that suppliers are not perfect, you must watch out for a supplier who botches multiple orders within a short time frame.

Chapter 5: What You Need to Start Your Dropshipping Business

Congratulations on getting this far! It's evident that you're not just keen on learning the ropes of dropshipping, but you're also determined to get started with your first dropshipping business. You already understand this business model and how easy it can be to not only get started but also run a successful and profitable business. This chapter takes you through all you need to get started. The reason for this is simple—while it's true that you don't need to break the bank for your initial capital, you must plan well and think ahead.

The Power of Having the Right Mindset

It's surprising how most people assume that all you need to run a successful dropshipping business is finances a site, a wholesaler, and sooner than later, you start selling and making a profit. What they don't know is that following this path only results in failure. This is the wrong approach to dropshipping. You need to shift your focus from making money to meeting a certain need/solving a problem. While it's true that you'll need certain resources and tools, you must learn some concepts in order to have the right mindset.

You can't underestimate the power of the right mindset because you also can't expect any success with your dropshipping business when you don't have the right mindset. You must take time to develop the right mindset because you set up your dropshipping business. This essentially means that you develop the mind of an entrepreneur; you're determined to make it work by embracing the right attitude. Some of the things you need to pay attention to that will help you to cultivate the right mindset for your dropshipping business include the following:

Willingness to Act

The entrepreneurial journey is characterized by numerous challenges that can dim your ambition to start your dropshipping business. In fact, it's common to find that you've done all the research you need but are afraid of making the bold move to hit the ground running because you're afraid of failure. In some cases, you could also find that you've spent so much time on research that you end up with the conviction that a dropshipping business is not a good idea for you, so you end up giving up. Having the mindset of taking action lets you act on the information you have gathered and turn it around to work to your advantage. You can seek perfection with time.

Flexibility

To succeed at your dropshipping business, you must have the flexibility of being able to tweak things if necessary in order to adapt to new situations. This is important because it's not every day that every move you make will yield results. You must be able to read the signs and make the necessary changes so as to maintain the general direction that your business should go. For instance, if you start out with a product that doesn't seem to attract customers, but a similar product seems to be on-demand, you can make a switch and adjustments to respond to the needs of the market.

Ability to Bounce Back

Ask any entrepreneur, and you'll be surprised by the number of times they failed before getting their business up. However, the distinguishing factor is how they responded to failure and bounced back. You must be ready to adjust to your circumstances as opposed to giving up whenever you face an obstacle. If you have the ability to bounce back, you will not give up when your first attempt at dropshipping fails. Instead, you will try a different approach or a different product altogether. It's this kind of mindset that will determine your longevity.

Things That You Need for Dropshipping

Here's what you need to start your dropshipping business:

Value Proposition

Before you can even think about finding suppliers, or even choosing a niche, think about value. Ironically, not so many people pay attention to value; rather, they focus on outselling competitors by offering cheap, low-quality products. Why is the value proposition important? This is what will set you apart from the competition. It's the key to setting up a successful business. When you prioritize value from the start, you'll get the attention of consumers and your business will last longer.

How, then, do you make value a priority? Well, you'll need to establish a number of things in order to make value your number one priority. First, have an idea of who it is that you want to help and what they want, identify a niche or niches that you can add value to, establish how to put your customers first, and finally, find the kind of products customers in the niche you've identifies want. To sum this up, you simply need to listen to your customers, know what they want, and give them. It's as simple as that. This will ensure you give your customers the best experience.

By emphasizing on value proposition, you'll have the right attitude that will see you realize several tangible benefits in your dropshipping business that include the ability to acquire and keep customers, you'll easily stand out from chocking competition (dropshipping can be overcrowded), and you're able to grow a customer base that is loyal to you. Value proposition also makes your business trustworthy and unique. Therefore, you'll do well to make value proposition a consistent theme in your dropshipping business.

Niche

If you've looked around keenly, you'll realize that so many dropshipping businesses fail even before they take off. Well, it can be discouraging to see retailers dropping out of business in their droves. But have you stopped to ask why this is usually the case? One of the mistakes that some of those who fail at dropshipping is selecting the wrong niche. Niche selection can either make or break your business. While there's no doubt that some niches are quite attractive, they are equally highly competitive. This means that in order to break through such niches, you must be able to cut through the noise and invest heavily in advertising to be able to compete against retailers who have been in the business for quite some time. This is no mean feat because you also need to add value at the same time. Since this is what your competitors are selling, you must take a different approach when adding value.

On the other hand, opting for a less popular niche could be a strategic move because you can meet a need/offer value in that niche without having to struggle to stand out from the competition. However, this doesn't mean that you don't have to work hard with the less crowded niches. Did you already have a niche in mind? Do you need to think again about it? Keep in mind identifying the right niche is more than just riding on the latest hottest trend. I talk about niche selection at length in chapter 7.

The Right Product

Apart from the value proposition and finding the right niche, you must have the right product. Are you wondering if there's anything like a wrong product? The right product is not necessarily a product that seems popular. You must be picky about product selection. To run a successful dropshipping business, make a careful selection of products while keeping in mind what your audience needs and wants. Even then, this alone is not enough, while at it, and think about the value of the product to your potential customers. Although you can begin by looking at the best-selling products in your quest to find the right products, this is not always a guarantee that you'll find. Instead, make sure the products have significant value to the customer. Products with lasting value are often a good bet because they don't go out of fashion easily, so you can be sure to sell them for the longest time.

Analyzing product trends is also a great move that you can use to find the right product. Having said that, aim at a strong start—meaning, find a product that will do well. For instance, if trends indicate that certain products have been popular in the past, and then chances are they sell quite well. Ultimately, understand that you don't have to stick to your initial choice of product, especially if it's not working for you. You can actually change your product line to respond to the needs of your audience. Make sure you're up to date with the latest trends in your niche and update your storefront to reflect this.

Supplier

Suppliers and wholesalers are a critical link in the dropshipping business because they help in executing your customer orders by shipping products directly to customers. When looking for suppliers, aim at finding suppliers who have a great reputation and a good communication channel. Finding a good supplier is important because it will determine several things like customer satisfaction, quality, and profit margins. Don't just choose the first supplier that you come across. You also don't want to choose a supplier because of their popularity in search engine results. Instead, approach your search with an open mind weighing your options and drawing price comparisons to make sure you get the products that you need. Above all, make sure that you know all the protocols you must follow when getting in touch with wholesalers and laying down the arrangements.

Registered Business

A majority of wholesalers and suppliers prefer to work with businesses that are legally incorporated. In most cases, wholesalers and suppliers will be hesitant to show you their pricing or even divulge more information when your business is not incorporated. The reason is simple; a dropshipping business is a business like any other. The only difference is the mode of operation. As such, it is guided by the same rules that govern traditional businesses. Failure to follow these rules and regulations could actually land you in trouble. Having a registered business name establishes you as a legitimate business.

Strategy

You need a vision and actionable strategy to implement it. While this is not to say that you should have a plan for every little thing you'll be doing, you need to have a plan for your business so that you know how to approach your business. This helps you to get a good sense of the big picture before you can figure out the finer details. Being thorough could just be what will take you to the next level. Some of the things that you must include in your strategy include how to get sales, the digital marketing strategies, taking an angle within your niche, and optimizing your online store for sales. You can ask tough questions so you can prepare for them. This will save you headaches and the possibility of failure in the future. When you have a plan for your business over a specified period, you're able to guide your vision because you'll be able to make the right move towards implementation and growing your business.

Finances

Although you'll not be holding an inventory, you need finances to take care of the basics before you can get started. The nature of dropshipping businesses is such that while a customer will purchase a product from your store, it will actually take some time before you can access the money. This is a kind of security measure that protects both the retailer and the buyer in a bid to prevent fraudsters from running away with money and failing to deliver a product. This means that you must have some money at hand to pay your supplier so that your customer receives the product before the funds from the purchase are remitted to you.

Unfortunately, most suppliers will demand advance payment before they can ship items to your customers. However, you could also talk to your supplier about purchase order financing so that you use the customer's order to finance the purchase of goods on credit and pay once you receive the money. The challenge with this option is that the supplier is also required to ship the item at an additional cost. Apart from having money to pay suppliers, you also need to pay for your e-commerce platform so that you have an online presence. This may be your own website or one of the many dropshipping sites like Shopify. This is not to say that you must have thousands of dollars to get started; rather, it will take time before your business grows gradually to handle orders worth $10,000 or more.

Permits and Licenses

The fact that the dropshipping business is virtual in nature makes it seem like an informal entity that doesn't require permits and licenses. In fact, it's not surprising that some dropshipping entrepreneurs don't take into account legal priorities only to end up getting surprised when suppliers ask them to provide copies of permits and licenses before they can do business with them. The fact that you're doing an online business means that you're making money from a financial activity like a traditional retailer; hence, you need to pay taxes. After all, you're taking part in the same activities as a traditional business except that you're doing it on a different model. Therefore, you should treat your dropshipping business like any other business entity that could benefit from formal registration. A license is important because it allows you to run your business in your city. Whether your business license if renewable bi-annually or annually, it generally shows that your business is operating within your jurisdiction for the purposes of taxation and regulation. Apart from a business license, you also must have a seller's permit that gives you the authority to collect tax on behalf of the government. Since you're likely to sell to customers across all the states, you should register to be able to collect taxes from those transactions, which you have, tax nexus. Today, nexus laws are changing to take care of transactions where the retailer is doing business in a state but doesn't have a physical address. An occupational permit is another must-have document because some of the suppliers will only want to partner with you when they can match the order with your shipping address. As such, you may find yourself in a situation where items are first shipped to you before you can ship them to the customer. Because it's likely that you'll be re-shipping the goods from your house, the home occupation permit lets you ship products to your customer from your house.

EIN Number

If you're setting up your dropshipping business in the U.S., you must apply for the Employer Identification Number (EIN) as required by the Internal Revenue Service. This is a requirement for all businesses. This number will be used as your dropshipping business's social security number. You will need it to file taxes, open a bank account for your businesses, apply for dropshipping accounts with wholesalers/suppliers, and do just about everything relating to operating your business. It's a little difficult to find a good dropshipping supplier when you don't have the EIN number.

Sales Tax

The payment of taxes in the dropshipping business is often overlooked, yet it's a complex process. This is because, as a retailer in the dropshipping model, it's incumbent upon you to submit taxes. This process is quite complicated, owing to a number of issues that include product sourcing, dropshipper location, customer locations, and the sales tax nexus. The tax nexus refers to the requirement for businesses that conduct business in a state to not only collect but also pay taxes on the sales that originate from the same state. This means that if you sell goods in Michigan, then you need to file and pay your taxes in Michigan. Unfortunately, the dropshipping model carries a very high risk relating to sales tax errors.

Some of the things you need to know about collecting taxes include:

Make sure you collect sales from the customer when you have nexus in the state where the sale took place. The only exception is when the transaction is considered tax-exempt.

If both you and the supplier didn't have nexus in the state when the transaction took place, you don't have an obligation to pay taxes. Instead, it's the customer who has an obligation to remit taxes, except where the sale is tax-exempt.

In the case where your supplier has nexus in the state where the sale took place, but you don't, then the supplier has the responsibility of collecting tax. Even then, this is not an absolute rule because different states approach it differently.

Marketing Plan

You need to have a comprehensive marketing plan before you can launch your business. Marketing is the key driver of running your online businesses. This will help you to put products in front of potential customers. You need to let people know about the products you're selling, and this requires a comprehensive marketing plan. This will serve as a blueprint for your business; therefore, make sure that it's actionable and realistic. Avoid lofty goals because it'll be impossible to achieve them. Your marketing plan should capture online marketing strategies like search engine optimization, social media marketing, content marketing, video marketing, video marketing, blogging, banner ads, and advertising, among others.

Chapter 6: How to Choose the Best E-Commerce Solution

Congratulations! You've made it this far and are now equipped with most of the information you need to start your first dropshipping business. However, before you do that, it's important that you understand the various e-commerce solutions that are available for you to choose from. There are a number of factors you must take into consideration when choosing the best e-commerce solution for your dropshipping business. This is to ensure that you do not compromise exposure to your target market or even profit margins.

The general advice is that if you need to make more money, you're better off creating your own dropshipping website. While this is likely to take longer to build, you'll eventually make more money from it compared to any other platform. On the other hand, if all you want is to get a wide audience for your products, then you can think of platforms like eBay and Amazon even though the margins will be reduced significantly. You can also peg your choice of platform on your long-term goals. This helps you to clearly define how much control you want to have when selling your products over time.

Things to Consider When Choosing an E-Commerce Platform

Here are some of the factors you need to consider when selecting an e-commerce platform:

Payment and Pricing

This is the first thing you must take into account when looking for an e-commerce platform. Whether you're just starting out or you have a well-established offline enterprise. First, you must establish the amount of money that you'll be paying. Most of the e-commerce platforms charge a monthly fee. This fee will vary from one platform to the other, depending on whether it's a self-hosted or a hosted platform. While you may be tempted to go for a lower price, make sure you're not compromising on other things that are more important. Take time to weight on the cons and pros of each of these platforms and go for what is best for your budget. You also need to consider how customers will be paying for goods purchased from your store. Not all platforms allow payments from third-party vendors like PayPal. This can end up being an inconvenience for your customers that eventually results in card abandonment. You shouldn't take this risk; instead, establish the forms of payment that the vendor will accept before making a decision.

Mobile-friendliness. Research shows that about 60 percent of all Internet searches are done on mobile devices. Some of these translate to a purchase. This means that you must look for platforms that will allow your customers to access your website easily as well as proceed to make a purchase using their mobile device. Shopify is one such example.

Integrations

It's also important to consider the e-commerce platform's integration and plugins. The majority of these platforms, such as Shopify, offer a host of tools that enable the smooth running of your business. You need to determine the plugins that will work best for your business by looking at what tools you need. Some of the most popular plugins that you need to consider include accounting plugins that will help you with revenues, taxes, sales and profits, email marketing tools that will help you when you want to contact your customers, a platform that rewards customers with some of your products and apps to help you when shipping.

Customer Service

Customer service is at the heart of every business. Traditional brick and mortar stores have an advantage over dropshipping because they have more control over how they run their business. On the other hand, you don't have too much control over your dropshipping business. You could experience software outages or server downtimes that are beyond your control, yet they prevent your customers from having a satisfaction-guaranteed experience. Unfortunately, the servers often crash at the worst times, and this can affect your brand image and revenue negatively. Thus, it's paramount that you have someone you can call at any time to help you get things up and running again. Consider every platform's customer service to determine its availability around the clock. You should be able to reach them with ease.

SEO Friendliness

Your dropshipping business isn't exempt from practicing SEO. In fact, SEO can be highly beneficial to work at having your store rank high in search engine results. You want your customers to find you easily when looking for products like yours. Some of the most important factors when looking for an SEO friendly platform include the ability to use your domain name, the ability to add a blog to your website, and the ability for customers to leave reviews of your site.

Scalability

When you're starting your business, you have goals of scaling it. After all, it's every business owner's desire to see your business grow. Therefore, it's important to find a platform that will allow you to scale your business. You shouldn't pay for features and storage that you're not using. Instead, you should be able to keep up with the increasing business demands without having to pay outrageous fees.

Security

There's no customer who wants to enter their credit card information on a website that is sketchy. Security is among the biggest concerns for most consumers. Although most software offers robust security as a standard, always check your e-commerce platform to make sure it supports HTTPS/SSL for a secure and safe checkout for your customers. Ensure that any platform that you will select is Payment Card Industry (PCI) compliant.

E-Commerce Platforms to Consider

Overall, you need to find an e-commerce solution that takes care of all your needs without compromising on the most basic of things. Let's look at some of the e-commerce sales platforms that you can consider:

Amazon

Among the common e-commerce solutions, Amazon seems like an obvious and easy choice. Partly, this is because it's one of the biggest online marketplaces globally and a platform of preference by most dropshippers. Did you know that most of the products listed on the Amazon website are sold by third-party merchants? It's important to critically look at this platform before making a decision or just flowing with the masses. The truth is that while Amazon has its share of advantages, it's not devoid of issues. While it many offer convenience, it's also likely to be detrimental to drop shippers. Let's take a quick look at the pros and cons of dropshipping on Amazon:

Pros of Amazon Dropshipping

- *It's trustworthy.* Most people treat Amazon like the standard for dropshipping. They view it more like a local big box store even as shopping on this platform has become a casual affair with most people buying their products here. As such, the chances are that your customers may already be regular visitors to the Amazon site for most of their purchases.

- *It has access to a wide audience.* Amazon boasts of receiving millions of visitors are any given time. This means that by listing your products on this site, you will instantly have access to these millions of people, something that you'd have to spend years and resources to achieve if you were to dropship on your own website. Amazon guarantees you reasonable traffic regardless of the products you're selling.

- *You're entitled to Fulfillment by Amazon (FBA).* Fulfillment by Amazon requires retailers to ship products to Amazon, who then ship them out to customers. This is especially good because it can give you additional revenue when you have your own products. While FBA is not a huge perk, it's definitely nice to have.

Cons of Amazon Dropshipping

- *Amazon charges a substantial listing fee.* Unfortunately, Amazon charges hefty fees for listing with them. This is usually in the range of 10 to 15 percent. This is in addition to the monthly base fee of $39.99. This is not good if your margins are already too low, as it will cut into your profits significantly. This is the cost you have to pay to enjoy access to the millions of potential buyers.

- *The payment method is not friendly for all.* There are two main challenges facing Amazon payment methods. For starters, they don't accept payments made via PayPal. This is a big deal considering how many people prefer using PayPal. Secondly, the payment system for merchants is such that they can only be paid every two weeks, which is not convenient for businesses.

- *The competition is stiff.* The popularity of this platform is an advantage and a disadvantage, too. While on the one hand, it gives you access to an incredible audience; on the other hand, it means stiff competition from other buyers. This is further compounded by the fact that buyers can automate their listings to adjust their prices to be the lowest hence most preferred by buyers. This results in pricing wars that are bad for most sellers because undercutting your competition is in no way a good practice rather a big problem.

eBay

eBay is another massive e-commerce platform that is trusted by millions of people who prefer using it for their shopping. This platform has so many similarities to eBay, with the two sites having the same advantages. However, the difference is that eBay is also an auction site. This platform can be invaluable for dropshippers who are starting out even though it comes at a price.

Pros of eBay Dropshipping

Easy to set up. It's easy to set up your dropshipping store on eBay. In fact, you can manage everything by yourself with little experience. You don't need to have team members to help you. Most importantly, eBay makes the processing of payments and handling finances a lot easier.

- *It's big.* One of eBay's selling points is its size. Just like Amazon, setting your dropshipping store on this e-commerce platform will grant you instant access to millions of probable customers who are ready to make purchases. This translates to little marketing so that you put more effort into leveraging the platform to work for you.

- *It's trustworthy.* Customers do trust eBay, owing to its solid seller protection policies that are attractive to new dropshippers. Most buyers will not hesitate to purchase from new buyers because they know they're covered in the event that something goes wrong. This means that it's easy to make your first sale and build on your online reputation.

Cons of eBay Dropshipping

- *The auction-style isn't great for dropshipping.* A conventional dropshipping site lets you list your product for as long as you're selling it. On the other hand, eBay's auction option means that you can only keep your listing up for a certain period. Your listings will eventually expire—after which, you have the option of relisting them. This can be time-consuming and inconvenience at the same time.

- *It's limiting.* There's so much you can't do with eBay. For instance, you cannot design your own storefront or build an email list. You must play by the platform's rules; hence, you will, in most cases, be stuck. Thus, you're unlikely to get repeat customers. You also can't build an audience or even a brand yourself. This can be quite frustrating because it makes it harder for you to stand out from your competition since all stores have the same look.

- *The fees can add up.* eBay has a bad reputation for high fees. This e-commerce platform takes up to 10 percent for every sale and sometimes even more. These fees are considered a necessary evil and a trade-off for selling on such a platform even though it doesn't dissuade some entrepreneurs from choosing eBay as a dropshipping platform.

Setting Up Your Own Website

Although it doesn't present you an opportunity to get your inventory before millions of customers, having your own website for your dropshipping business offers you a number of advantages that you won't get from other platforms. While having your own site gives you a lot of freedom, you must be willing to make some compromises. Setting up your dropshipping website will be overwhelming when you don't have prior experience. However, you'll be surprised by how easy it is when you have software like Shopify. You can easily create your site and integrate an e-commerce plugin to make your site.

Advantages of Setting up Your Own Dropshipping Website

- *You don't have to pay outrageous fees.* When you set up your own website, there are no third parties involved who would take a cut, thus affecting your profit margins. You don't have to pay the 10 or 15 percent fees eBay or Amazon charges. All you need to worry about is payment processing fees and the cost of products.

- *You can stand out.* All the Amazon and eBay pages look the same. Having your own website allows you to implement your unique branding and make a lasting impression on your website visitors. This usually makes a big difference because it helps you to build your brand and draw loyal repeat customers.

- *It's easier to create a mobile responsive store.* Making a purchase via your mobile device is not always a pleasant experience, especially where the site is not optimized for mobile. This can result in an abandoned cart. When you have your own dropshipping website, you are able to make a responsive site for your customers. This also makes it possible to manage your business from your phone and keep an eye on your business on the go.

- *You have total control.* When you have your own store, you make decisions concerning everything you want to include in your store—from where you'll place the logo to the format of your pages. Moreover, you're able to communicate your value to your readers, which can give you an edge over your competitors.

Disadvantages of Setting Up your Own Dropshipping Website

- *It takes time before it can pick up.* Since you don't have a ready audience, you have to market your store aggressively. This means that it'll take time before you can begin seeing traffic or even make your first sale.

- *You don't have access to a large audience.* Having your own site means you must be ready to build your audience from the ground up. This means you must be willing to put in money, time as well as effort to generate traffic and outreach.

Chapter 7: Niche Product or Not?

One of the biggest first decisions you'll have to make is the choice of product to offer through your dropshipping storefront. This is not an easy pick because it narrows down to the niche. Careful selection of a niche is the key to your dropshipping success. While niche selection may seem like a straightforward affair, it's actually complicated. Remember, you need to select a profitable niche that is not too crowded with stiff competition. Thus, you must take some time to research and analyze a niche from the perspective of a retailer to determine whether you'd be successful in that particular niche. You can begin with multiple niches and eventually narrow down to a specific niche.

It can be tempting to jump straight into the seemingly hottest trends and nice and just set up your store in a matter of hours. Actually, many dropshippers follow this approach only to end up being very frustrated. Refrain from joining the bandwagon because you're motivated by runaway success because your business will fall apart. This accounts for the high rate of dropshipping businesses that fall apart. Make sure you select your niche carefully in order to set up a business that will grow steadily and develop an impressive income stream. Your choice of niche determines everything else concerning your business that includes the products you'll offer, how much you will sell the products for, your choice of suppliers, the marketing strategies you'll use, and the ultimate success of your business. That's why dropshippers who realize a niche that they selected isn't working go back to the drawing board to begin the process all over again. Generally, your success will come from asking the right questions.

Identifying a Niche

Identifying a niche lets you find the 20% of customers that will account for 80% of your profit. There are many niches you can consider from fashion products to pet supplies, organic food products, baby clothes, and electronic goods, among others. When you have a niche, you can then narrow down to a specific section of the market that you will focus on. It's much better to focus on a particular demographic that target everyone.

You must be able to identify and ascertain the viability of a niche before you set up your business. This process can be stressful, yet it helps to draw the line between success and failure. Don't rely on commerce experts or even online courses because they are never thorough and can't be relied upon. When considering a niche, try and balance between uniqueness and the potential to make a profit. You can begin by brainstorming to identify the gaps in the market and products that are being offered. Only then can you begin actual research. Various platforms let you carry your research to be able to find the right niche. They include the following:

- *Trend Hunter*. This uses big data to offer reliable market intelligence that is up to date. This website carries out detailed market research before making recommendations on the product ideas based on purchase patterns and consumer interest. You can leverage these listings to find a product by drawing comparisons between the trending products on the Trend Hunter website and those that are featured on Shopify, among other dropshipping sites. By following this approach, you will always identify trends before other people within the dropshipping community discover them.

- *Dropshipping sites*. Taking a look at the dropshipping stores is a good way of identifying a niche as well as products that have a high demand and those with very few retailers selling them. Some dropshipping sites are particularly insightful because you can gather so much information that will help you to make the right decision.

- *Google trends.* The Internet has made it possible to access information at the click of a button. You can begin your search for a perfect niche with a Google search. You just may be surprised by the search results. However, if all you can find is everyone selling just about the same thing, you need to venture deeper into your search. Google Trends is analytic in nature; hence, it allows you to evaluate items against the Google database. You can use it to determine the popularity of products or even compare the popularity of different products to determine how they perform against the competition.

- *Instagram.* This social networking site has the capacity to offer great ideas for niche products. People are always posting on Instagram under multiple hashtags. You can use the keywords of the products you have in mind and see the results that come up. If you realize that many people have the desire to own something that is a sign of an unfulfilled market.

- *Facebook.* Once you have brainstormed on the various products, you can look up some of the Facebook forums that are associated with your niche of interest. This will give you an opportunity to interact with like-minded individuals and even ask questions. If you notice that a group is dormant or has low interaction, it could probably mean there isn't much demand for business in that niche.

Evergreen Niche Products

There are certain products that people will always spend money on. They include lifestyle products like collectibles, movies, and comic books, among others that are usually on demand almost all year round. These are considered to be evergreen niche products. They include the following:

- *Hobbies and sports*. The fitness craze continues to be sustained; hence, the number of people purchasing home gym supplies keeps on soaring. The same goes for weight loss products.

- *Gaming*. Gamers are always looking out for the next item they can celebrate their hobby with. If you can tap into this niche, then you can be sure to keep the sales going.

- *Beauty*. This is another popular e-commerce market. Dropshippers sell products worth billions every year with most of the beauty products selling worldwide. This only gets better with a growth in population because the market will expand.

- *Home security.* This is another emerging niche with great potential. It comes with multiple sub-niches as new products are constantly being launched.

- *Fashion.* People will always be fascinated by fashion products, so you can never go wrong with this niche. You only need to be strategic.

Evaluating Your Dropshipping Niche Ideas

Choosing your dropshipping niche can be a challenge because you can't easily tell which one is viable. Besides, there are thousands of businesses in just about every niche, so you're not certain about how you'll identify a profitable niche. Some niches may seem to be saturated when they actually open for product purchasing options. Yet other niches have not been tapped into exhaustively. So how then can you tell a good niche apart from one that is overcrowded or lacks potential? What criteria should you use to find this niche? Well, niche evaluation is a complex process, but there are simple tactics you can employ to choose a niche within a short duration. Determining the suitability of a niche will be based on three things; the level of competition, long term projection of the popularity of the niche, and demand for physical products in the niche.

The ideal dropshipping niche is one that has medium or low competition with a potential for high demand. Additionally, it will be popular. Unfortunately, it's almost impossible to find such a niche. It's upon you to figure out the right balance that is usually varied from one person to the other. If you're uncertain about where to begin your search, consider this two-step process:

Step 1: Find Trending or Niches with Low Competition

A simple search for trending niche or even low competition niches will generate thousands of search engine results. This will give you a big picture of a number of dropshipping niches making it a good place to start. This search will lead you to niches that are trending as well as those that are projected to become popular over time. The challenge with these is that despite the immense potential they have, they can get overcrowded. On the other hand, while low competition niches seem to be perfect since they're not too crowded, they could limit the amount of money you can make because they usually have a smaller customer base. Therefore, you want to be sure that the niche you selected meet the following criteria:

Is the Niche Product-Based?

It's important to establish whether the niche has a reasonable number of products linked to it. Some niches don't have products, for instance, those that deal in digital products, making them unsuitable for dropshipping. As you carry on with your search for the appropriate niche, you'll realize that some of the niches have more products than others, making them better than others. That is, the more products you can offer, the better. While the idea is not to sell just about everything there is in that niche—it's better when you have a variety. For this reason, a niche with many products is a good bet for your dropshipping business as it offers room for expansion and growth. Even then, high product variety also means high competition. Thus, you may also want to look at niches that are not too competitive but have a good product variety.

Another important consideration is the ease of access to these products for both yourself and your customers. For instance, it's not easy to dropship custom made items. Moreover, they'll not give you a good profit margin. Moreover, some of the obscure products will not just have a broad appeal. A product that appeals to many people is likely a good product to dropship.

The Popularity of the Niche

Generally speaking, your goal is to find a niche that isn't too popular yet has sufficient interest and excellent product demand that can sustain your retail business. In most cases, you'll have to come to a compromise; therefore, you need to know when and how to compromise. When researching a niche and find a niche that is extremely popular, it should serve as a warning sign that it may be too difficult to break into this niche. The reason is simple, with the competition being high, you'll have challenges getting noticed; thus, you're better of settling for a niche that isn't highly competitive. Are you panicking already? You shouldn't because following the two-step niche evaluation strategy will help you to identify an excellent niche that isn't too crowded.

Check That the Niche Is Not Just a Passing Trend

It's common to have a handful of trends coming and going every year. Interestingly, businesses will come up and take advantage of these trends. When the trend fizzles, the businesses also follow suit. However, you can't dismiss trends entirely because some of the trends end up becoming the next big thing. For instance, niche products like virtual reality gear, fidget spinners, and drones became big over time, and the dropshippers who have tapped into this niche made a kill from the sales. Even then, the risk is higher when you opt for a niche because of its popularity. Therefore, it's safe when you choose a niche that has been around for some time. A relatively new niche is not always a good idea, but you can opt to evaluate it on a case by case basis.

How Passionate Are You About the Niche?

Generally, having passion is a good thing. However, having too much passion can be a setback for your dropshipping business. The reason is simple—passion doesn't always translate into sales. You need to sell products that will attract customers to buy and become a sustainable career over time. Passion obscures your reasoning so that you don't see the realities of operating a business, so you find that you are just keeping products even though they're not selling. So if you have passion about a certain niche, you also must know when to detach yourself and make sober decisions. This means that you can opt for a favorite niche only if you can make objective evaluation so that you only go for it out of merit. You can also get an outside view to inform your decision. Most importantly, look through the entrepreneurial lenses so that you base your decision on figures and facts without involving your emotional side.

Will You Add Value to the Niche?

Most people assume that by opening a dropshipping store, you'll be doing value addition. This is not true. Instead, you should understand that you're not just offering a product but value. If you focus on offering value, you're likely to find it easy getting customers and eventually building your dropshipping business. Value is everything; therefore, you need to emphasize on value and put your customers first. This creates the best conditions that allow your business to thrive. When your focus is not on the value proposition, you'll definitely find it difficult making a sale. This calls for you to be very honest with yourself and ask if you can add value to the niche, or you can offer something different to customers who already have a sea of retailers to choose from. This leads up to the next step that is looking up for retailers in the niche.

Step 2: Look Up Existing Retailers

This step is as important as the first in your search for a profitable niche. Take time to search for retailers that already have a footing in a particular niche. You can do this by using a number of combinations of product keywords to find who is selling, what they're selling, and also identify the retailers who seem to dominate. You can capture vital information like their names, social handles, and website on a spreadsheet. Look up the most and least popular stores as well as everything in between. This is because some of the smaller dropshippers are gaining popularity by simply doing something unique. Thus, analyzing them is as important as analyzing big retailers.

Make sure you capture as much information as possible so that you're able to understand their strategies for success. When you know what it is that they're doing, you'll be able to apply the knowledge to your situation. Make sure you pay attention to the store's online presence as well as the social media accounts so that you understand the strategies. Here, you'll be looking at the kind of content the retailers' posts, when they mention the products they're selling, and the manner through which they engage customers to learn a thing or two from them. If you're not able to find as many retailers, it could be a red flag. Here's why low competition is great. However, you need to have a significant audience to purchase your niche products. Low activity on a niche could be a sign that the niche is a bad choice, or it doesn't have a wide variety of products. Although this step is not the ultimate determiner of the niche you'll choose, it gives you an idea of what you'll be dealing with if you opt for it. It also helps you realize the kind of value you could give to your customers. At the end of this process, you should have a list of niches that are an excellent choice for dropshipping.

Unsaturated or Saturated Niche?

If you wanted a perfect niche, it would be one with low competition but a large audience. Unfortunately, this is hardly the case in reality. A typical niche will be moderately saturated with a relatively high number of retailers and a sizeable audience. Coming to a point where you have to choose between a supersaturated and a super unsaturated niche can be a tough call to make. Even then, it is rare to have to choose between these two options because most of the time, you'll find a niche that isn't completely unsaturated or saturated. In the event that these are the only choices you have to make, you should go back to the drawing board and consider your initial niche ideas. You can hardly run a profitable business when the niche has extensive competition. So it is difficult to be profitable in a niche that hardly generated interest from customers. While this possibility is rare, thinking about it lets you adjust your mindset so that you're not only focused on making a profit that you ignore other important factors and end up with a wrong niche.

Sustainability of the Niche

It's critically important to consider is the niche you're interested in is sustainable or not. Once you're certain that the niche is not a fad and has the potential of blowing over in a matter of time, you need to begin thinking about the future. Having a long-term perspective can be the difference between failure and success. While most niche products may seem great for dropshipping presently, however, thinking about them in terms of timelines like a year from now, then you can be able to tell whether it's a promising niche or not.

For instance, if you're considering the phone accessories niche, it will not be surprising to see that this is a saturated niche. However, from a futuristic point of view, people will always have phones. In fact, the number of people who own phones may increase. Moreover, they'll also want to decorate their phones. This qualifies this niche for sustainability. On the other hand, if the eclipse is just about to happen, you could quickly set up a dropshipping store to sell various gears. This may seem easy, but the eclipse is not a regular occurrence, so you'll only be getting sales during the years when the eclipse occurs. This makes it a poor and unsustainable niche choice. When you consider sustainability, think about the lifespan of the niche. Will the niche be as popular one year down the line? What about five years? This is not easy to figure out because it can be difficult to predict the future.

Closing a Sale

By the time your dropshipping business becomes functional, you will be having just about everything you need to make a sale. From suppliers to manufacturers, you'll be ready to start making income. You might be a little anxious about what your first sale will be like. But this is normal. What you need to keep in mind is that today, most people are not patient when it comes to the time it takes before they receive the product. In fact, the fastest way to lose a sale is the inability to deliver products to your customers quickly and in an efficient manner. Today, people prefer to receive their products right away. Therefore, you must be able to supply and deliver customer purchases when the customer expects it. Since you're relying on your supplier to fulfill your customer orders, make sure you're working with a supplier that is capable of handling orders expeditiously so as to meet the needs of your customers.

Make sure the shipping terms are clearly outlined in your store's terms and conditions so that you're not bringing up last-minute fees the customer was not expecting during checkout. This is a great way of ensuring customer satisfaction. Additionally, make sure you provide accurate information where there are delays necessitating that orders go out after a day. You can also consider working with more than one supplier to help in handling orders as well as ensure the availability of products. Most importantly, this solves problems with availability and shipping.

Even then, sealing a deal and closing a sale takes time and focus. With so many ways and channels to promote your business, you can find yourself constantly tweaking your store to perfect it in a bid to get people to come to your store. Here's what you need to do to close your first sale:

- *Get targeted traffic.* As a new store owner, you may get caught up with changing fonts, colors, and even second-guessing prices and assumes you're making progress. Well, while all these are important, you need to work on driving targeted traffic to your store to get exposure for your business. Traffic lets you know if there's interest in your products, if the prices are reasonable and if your brand resonates with your target audience.

    You can begin with free traffic sources where you share your store manually with your online communities and network. As you tackle free traffic sources, you can consider a number of things, which include offering a discount coupon to entice customers; adding your store's URL to your personal profiles on social media accounts like Twitter, Instagram, or even Disqus profile of blog comments;

avoiding spamming audiences with low quality, repetitive promotional messages; and joining online communities and becoming an active member. All these give you an opportunity to share your store, build connections, and eventually get to send customers to your store. You can also use paid advertising where you're basically spending money to make money. Most of these are usually pay per click based, so you don't need to have a big budget to get paid traffic. Some of the best platforms where you can sign up for paid traffic include Facebook, Instagram advertising, Pinterest marketing, and Google Ads.

- *Do an outreach.* Although you should the number 1 champion for your business, you also need to get other people talking about your store and products. This may mean reaching out to bloggers for partnership in writing guest posts, product reviews, or even pitching news stories. You can also seek strategic partnerships to get your products to be seen by someone else's customers. You can run a contest, package samples your product or give exclusive discounts, sponsor an event, or even create a product together. Influencer marketing has come up very strong, so you can take advantage and work with influencers to promote and push your products to their legion of followers. Lastly, you don't have to drive all traffic online; you can take your marketing campaign offline by adopting guerrilla marketing that involves a combination of creativity and guts.

- *Analyze, reflect back, and optimize.* Once you've tried all the tactics and have seen a jump in traffic, you need to analyze the traffic, diagnose potential problems and optimize your store for sale—that is, look at some of the reasons why customers are not buying from you, analyze the high bounce rate, why visitors are not adding products to their cart, and the abandoned cart rate. With all this information at hand, you can tweak things about your store so you'll have a better chance to get buyers to purchase. Sooner than later, you'll make your first sale.

Overall, it's not difficult to make a sale on your dropshipping store. You just need to get your marketing strategy on point.

Chapter 8: Dropshipping Marketing Strategies to Increase Sales

Opening a dropshipping store and beginning dropshipping is one of the easiest ways you can earn money. However, setting up your store is just the beginning. With so many other dropshippers yearning for the same attention from would-be buyers, you must work on your marketing strategy to not only drive traffic to your store but also convert visitors to buyers. Your dropshipping store is nothing if you don't have customers.

Here are some tested dropshipping marketing strategies you can use for your store:

Design a Terrific Interface for Your Store to Attract Customers

You can't overlook the power of first impressions. The first impression a visitor will have on your store will determine whether they'll do business with you or not. The first impression could be made based on your store design. The design of your site should encourage visitors to embrace your brand and products without having to scroll through the site endlessly. Make sure you don't have clutter and useless content on your homepage. You should also ensure customers can navigate through your catalog with ease. Most importantly, include a search button and make sure it's prominent. Making sure your dropshipping store is mobile responsive is another great way you can take advantage of mobile traffic so that you're not losing potential customers.

Social Media Integration

Social media lets you share content in various formats, which can greatly complement your other marketing channels, thus improving sales significantly. It's unlikely that your dropshipping business will thrive without the integration of social media, which will make your marketing ineffective. Apart from creating an account on social media platforms, you can also leverage influencer marketing to send you traffic that will convert into sales because they have recommended a product you're selling to their fans.

Email Marketing

This entails sending a commercial message to an individual or group of people via email. This can include business requests, advertisements, or creating brand awareness. An effective email marketing campaign is able to provide you an incredible number of visitors and, subsequently, sales.

However, you must make sure your email marketing campaigns are written skillfully enough to catch the attention of the most cramped inboxes. Remember, email marketing is one of the most effective techniques for email markers. Email marketing is cost-effective because you don't need a huge budget for printing, postage, or even adverting fees. All you need is an active email address. Moreover, it lets you reach out to a targeted audience because when customers make a purchase, you can capture their demographics and interests. This helps to eliminate a situation where you're spending too much on advertising that has fewer returns. Email marketing is great when you want to measure the success of your business. It's essential for gathering data to determine the movement of sales even as you track customer's behavior and interests. These can then inform your marketing strategy so that you emphasize more on those products that customers are more interested in.

Cross Selling and Upselling Products

Cross-selling and upselling products involve introducing your customers to complementary or better products compared to what they're interested in. This marketing strategy is often better than the acquisition of new customers because when done well, you can be guaranteed a repeat customer.

Engaging Customers via a Live Chat

Having a live chat feature allows you to hold conversations with your visitors so you are able to answer or address any concerns they may be having that could be hindering them from making a purchase decision. Although this means that you'll have to put in more effort, it produces a high impact. If anything, not all customers will want to engage you in the live chat feature. This function will be particularly handy if you're selling products with a high price range.

Content Marketing

This is a simple but very effective way of taking your business to the next level. Content marketing lets you address any questions that visitors to your site may be having in addition to helping you rank better in search engines. Even then, understand that content marketing not only limited to blogging; you could consider other options that include a video, a podcast, or even a free e-book.

A Customer Loyalty Program

Offering a loyalty program serves as an incentive that allows your customers to make a purchase. Loyalty programs also help in keeping your brand on opting as the customers' minds via automated reminders. Having a loyalty program will encourage repeat customers to your store. This can be anything from redeeming point, membership points, or whatever you can think about to entice customers to come back repeatedly.

Dropship Private Label Products

The best way to market your dropshipping store and products it to make sure you're selling the best products. As the dropshipping industry becomes more competitive, you'll need to make sure that your business stays thrives. You can achieve this by venturing into private label products. You could also consider selling private label products in order to increase your sales significantly. Dropshipping private label products is an excellent marketing strategy that is guaranteed to increase your sales. Here are some of the advantages of dropshipping private label products:

- **Exclusivity promotion** - Private label products will no doubt separate you from your competitors. Private label products give you an exclusive feel, especially when you're selling products because you have an opportunity to stand out from your competition. When you market these products and create demand for it, you will become the only supplier with the product your customers prefer for sale. Moreover, you can easily charge premium prices on your products because you have an exclusive feel. You'll be surprised at how much people are willing to buy private label products compared to the price of similar products that are much cheaper.

- **Better profit margins** - Dropshipping private label products are one of the strategies you can use to achieve higher profit margins. Private label products help you to have a lower cost basis for products, thus allowing you to gain more in profit than you'd usually do selling products that your competitors are also selling. Private label products fetch stronger profit margins that help to balance out the smaller gains.

- **Wholesale income** - You can also promote exclusivity by operating as a wholesaler. This gives other dropshippers an opportunity to pay premium prices just to be able to carry your brand. This eventually helps in generating income while allowing your brand to gain more exposure over time. This may also be in the form of a referral or affiliate program that lets you gain more sellers for your products.

- **Brand loyalty** - Building a loyal customer base is one of the pillars of the long-term success of your dropshipping business. Branding your products is an effective means of enhancing customer loyalty. This is a great move as long as your audience gets value from these products. Having a private label will make your customers have an attachment to your brand. This helps in evoking feelings because they are among the few people who own them. This strategy will work well if you're selling high-end products.

How to Start Dropshipping Private Label Products

Before you start dropshipping private label products, you need to ensure that you start by building your brand effectively. Here are several ways through which you can begin dropshipping private label products:

- *Research the products you'll sell.* There's a wide range of products you can sell as private label products. They include cosmetics and skincare products, electronics, tools, fashion accessories, and apparel, among others. There are many more products you can sell as private label products, but the challenge is ensuring they're profitable. This means you must be willing to research more on consumer demand and the cost of potential competitors. This is because they play an important role when you want to have a profitable product. To limit the loss and ensure profitability, you need to make sure that you need to test the product first. This means you sell some of the items without branding them first; then, you private-label the best sellers. In the meantime, you can use customized packaging or bags to brand your store and build customer loyalty.

- *Conduct research on popular products with Google AdWords.* If you don't know the products that you're likely to sell, you can take advantage of Google's keyword finder tool. This gives you a peek into the number of people that are searching for particular terms on the Internet. You can use this to gauge and determine the demand for potential products you can sell under private labels. Make sure the item you intend to sell is generating high search engine traffic. Otherwise, it will not be worth selling because you'll have a difficult time selling.

- *Work with a reliable wholesaler.* Although private label drop shipping will offer you an expanded market, it's important to make sure you partner with a wholesaler with a good reputation. Overlooking this factor will only leave you struggling when it comes to marketing your private label products due to quality issues as well as shipping time and packaging. Getting into a partnership with a reliable supplier also gives you the ability to focus your efforts on promotion, sales, and profits.

The dropshipping market is quite competitive today, so you need to do whatever you have to stay relevant. When you create your own brand, you will build customers' trust, making them come back for more.

Checking Your Competition

The fact that you have implemented marketing strategies is not a guarantee that you will be at the top. You must keep in mind that your competitors are also working overdrive to get their businesses to the top spot. It's even more competitive if you're dropshipping on Amazon or eBay because your competition is on the same site as you. In fact, customers are unlikely to realize just how many different providers are available. You may have to consider moving away from the pack and offer a product that most of your competitors are not offering. Although you'll not be able to get ahead of all your competitors, your site will be a little different, giving customers a reason to choose you over your competition.

You can leverage Google and Google trends to see if the items you're thinking of offering are actually being searched. Google Trends will offer free information on the number of searches, where they are originating from, as well as how these searches are trending. This data is important because it helps to determine the popularity of the products. When you have this information, you will make your decision from an informed point of view. It's even better when you know the kind of product you'd like to sell because you can narrow down your product offerings on Google Trends along with the keywords that are associated with them. When you use SEO to narrow down the keywords, you will get a useful analysis of data that will contribute to increased traffic to your site. You could consider having products that are not very popular hence are unlikely to be found in large retailers' stores. You can use Google Trends to narrow your niche as well as determine how you will market your site to specific audiences. You can obtain data on the number of searches that have been conducted for specific products over a specified period. You can even narrow down to geographical regions so that you differentiate those regions that are showing interest in your products from those that are not. This is important because it allows you to fine-tune your SEO so that your site only appears in feeds of those people who are interested in what you're selling.

You can also use Google Trends to capture data on related products that people are searching for other than the keywords you're using for SEO. This is a great way to find other items that you may want to include in your niche.

Owing to the fact that you're dropshipping, you need to make sure you can source the item from your existing suppliers. This makes it possible to ship the items together. It also offers you the opportunity to bundle items together and create a unique package that will be attractive to your customers leading to increased revenue and repeat traffic. You can also look for your competitors' Google Trends to get a glimpse into what they are selling as well as where they're focusing their market share. It's good to have this information because it lets you know the trends you should be focusing on and what markets are getting crowded. You can also tell where your traffic is originating from, whether it's Google search, Instagram, or Facebook. You can then get insight on how to market your dropshipping store.

It's easier to create business accounts on Instagram and Facebook. You can also consider paying for ads placement on pages of people who have an interest in your niche. This will help you in generating more sales for your business. Facebook is becoming even better at advertising because of the way they generate revenue by selling ad space. You will do well to take action on the research data by maximizing the keywords grouped into a phrase and long-tail keywords to obtain the right traffic for your site. You can make the most of your advertising budget by enhancing your ad placement in the feeds of Facebook groups of interested users. This also applies to Instagram, where you can visit your competitor's Instagram page to see the ads that are generating hits for them. This will give you an idea of the kind of photos that generate interest to ignite your creativity in presenting products on Instagram.

If you have an Amazon site, you should also consider the Amazon Keyword Tool in working out your SEO to generate keywords to link customers to your site. This can be quite instrumental in generating traffic for your site. To get the most of the Amazon Keyword tool, use the paid version to be able to find long-tail keywords that simply autofill your site when customers are searching on Amazon. Since Amazon is a large site with many sellers that are banking on the same customers, make sure you make use of these tools if you want to get ahead of your competition.

Creating Your Customer Database

Having a database of visitors coming to your site is a great idea because it helps you to collect data that you can use to inform your marketing efforts and grow your dropshipping business. You can give your site visitors the opportunity to sign into a database. You can achieve this by offering an email newsletter or another form of communication where visitors leave their emails freely. You can use your customer database to announce new products as well as offer discounts and coupon codes.

When you have a database, you have access to people who have expressed interest in your product niche. Customers who have already visited your site and have signed up to receive future communication from you are more likely to return to the site when you offer incentives. You need to offer customers an opportunity to sign up to receive emails with offers and incentives from you during checkout. This way, the customer will have an opportunity to return to your site. The signup could be incentivized by a discount off the next purchase using a coupon code you've provided.

You can also set up a short survey at the end of the purchase process. This provides you with insight into the customer experience on your site because most people hardly post it on the Internet. This is a great move because most people prefer not to post any reviews unless they are extremely impressed or unhappy with the experience they had. Therefore, a short survey may be a great way of determining how people feel concerning your store. It also offers them an opportunity to make suggestions on ways to improve your store. A survey is an excellent way of finding those customers who are undecided and encouraging them to make the purchase decision. When you attach the survey to a particular order, you will not only have a record of what the customer purchased but also have the opportunity to match it with a probability of upselling items that are in your inventory. While this could require more algorithms, it's definitely worth the effort and money. Your website will be recommending items that match what the customer has selected. These discounts can be communicated through email. You could also obtain customer information through mailing lists from a third party where the database is used for social media posts and emails. Alternatively, you can also purchase this same information but for those people that have never visited your site. However, this can only be an effective tool when you purchase more names so that you're able to generate traffic to your site. While companies that sell the mailing lists will claim to give you names of those who are interested in your niche, you need to keep in mind that it's a chance you're taking because they may or may not be interested after all.

Chapter 9: How to Dropship on Shopify

You can't talk about dropshipping exhaustively without mentioning Shopify. I'm sure you have encountered Shopify in the earlier chapters. But do you really know what it is? Well, let me simplify it; Shopify is the most prominent e-commerce platform that has enables thousands of entrepreneurs to set up their online stores. This platform is easy to use as it lets you build your dropshipping store even without technical expertise. This makes it a perfect option for entrepreneurs who want to start out without too much involvement. Moreover, it gives you access to a host of themes and apps so you can personalize and optimize your store for sales.

Why Should You Start Dropshipping with Shopify?

Like I mentioned earlier, Shopify is the most superior e-commerce platform you'll ever find. This platform is home to more than half a million entrepreneurs, which makes it likely that its features make it possible for them to succeed. Moreover, it offers the flexibility of being able to add apps to cater to all the needs of your store. Trust is another aspect that has also drawn entrepreneurs to the Shopify platform. You can trust this platform to stay up even on major holidays.

When you perform dropshipping on Shopify, you will not have to worry about excess inventory because you only order the number of products you need to meet the demand from your customers. This platform breaks away from other e-commerce set up that involves purchasing or manufacturing products from wholesalers in bulk. Thus, Shopify gives you a lot of control over your inventory with a couple of clicks.

Reasons Why Shopify Is Your Number One Pick for Financial Freedom

Shopify is a preferred choice for sellers who are looking for efficiency and quality, along with rich features and simplicity. This platform not only promises a perfect blend of functionality and aesthetics but also delivers it. Here are some top reasons why you should make Shopify your number one pick for financial freedom:

Visually Appealing

Shopify brings together various professional templates that come in handy in the creation of unique stores that are visually appealing. Although it comes with a bare minimum theme for those who don't want a sophisticated interface, you have the liberty to work on it to create a store that offers a rich user experience as well as an exceptional UX.

Easy to Set Up and Use

Shopify prides itself on being a no-fuss platform. This means that you can set it up and use it even when you don't have any technical experience. It's a great alternative when you want a complete solution, but you don't want to engage in technicalities relating to web development and hosting for your online store. The platform offers hosting as well as the relevant software required for you to launch your site. What's more? It comes with an intuitive and user-friendly admin interface that complements the compelling user interface.

Security and Reliability

Shopify offers you reliability and security. That is, as you process customer orders, you'll be handling their financial and confidential personal information as well. This is critical because you don't want instances where your customer's confidential data is compromised. Moreover, you want a platform that is always online, and Shopify takes care of these features well. In addition, it also gives room for upgrading and maintenance.

App Integration

Shopify offers customization capabilities that are second to none. This platform offers room for integrating apps whenever you want to introduce extra functionalities and features to your store as well as enhance its value.

Powerful Marketing Tools

Shopify is a complete platform that comes with a marketing advantage. The basic Shopify version comes along with advanced e-commerce analytics tools. The app store gives you access to a host of marketing tools for social media integration and product reviews. Other marketing tools include discount coupons, custom gift cards, target email marketing, store statistics, and so much more. The SEO features also let your site rank higher in search engine results, making it easier for customers to find you. Whenever you feel overwhelmed by marketing, you can take advantage of Shopify Kit that serves as a virtual employee by recommending as well as executing marketing tasks based on your store performance, audience, and products.

Excellent Loading Speed

As a global hosted solution, Shopify boasts of solid and reliable infrastructure that comes with optimized software and hardware. This gives the platform an incredibly fast loading speed such that the e-commerce store that is created on it also loads in a matter of seconds.

Outstanding Customer Support

Shopify gives you the flexibility of being able to offer your customers reliable, round the clock customer support. Besides, the Shopify experts are always on standby 24/7 via live chat, email, and phone to resolve any queries you may have so that your store keeps running flawlessly round the clock.

Mobile Responsiveness

Today a large percentage of people access the Internet via their phones. Shopify understands the importance of mobile responsiveness to the success of any e-commerce store, even as the number of mobile customers does increase. Thus, all the Shopify themes are mobile responsive—meaning that they can be used to create stores that are mobile optimized. Additionally, there are Android and iPhone apps you can use to manage your store.

Abandoned Cart Recovery

Statistics show that more than two-thirds of the potential customers are likely to visit a store, place items in the shopping cart, and leave without buying. Well, Shopify helps you to take care of the abandoned checkout cart by automatically tracking the customer and sending out an email to remind them to complete the purchase process. This enhances revenue generation for your store.

Pricing and Affordability

Generally speaking, the cost of a good e-commerce website is anywhere between $3,000 and $5,000. This cost is too high for startups. As an entrepreneur, you're always looking for an opportunity to reduce costs while maximizing profits. Shopify offers a pricing plan that is affordable for your store. The pocket-friendly prices have endeared Shopify to startups and established stores alike. Shopify pricing is based on a subscription model that requires you to pay a small monthly fee. This is definitely a good deal compared to the benefits you get for using this platform. Most importantly, should you get to a point where you want to leave the platform, you can use the internal system to sell your store.

Easy Payment Gateway

Although Shopify has incorporated a number of payment gateways, it also offers its own payment platform that is powered by Stripe. When you use this platform to accept payments, you'll not incur any transactional costs in addition to benefiting from lower credit card fees. Besides, you don't need to have a merchant account to use this service.

Using Shopify to Maximize the ROI

Having a Shopify store in itself doesn't guarantee sales. As a matter of fact, there are a handful of other drop shippers yearning for a piece of the same customers you're targeting. This means that you have to be smart enough to come up with marketing strategies that will increase your ROI.

In this section, I take you through a step-by-step guide to setting up your Shopify dropshipping store. I also show you some tips to guide you through every step to ensure that you have a functional Shopify store in the end. Here are the steps you need to follow to open your Shopify dropshipping store:

Name Your Dropshipping Store

This is the first thing you must do before you even create an account on the Shopify platform. To come up with a name for your store, you need to be creative, keep it simple, and make it memorable. Remember, there are numerous other stores vying for the attention of customers. Oberlo has made it easy for you to pick a name for your store using their online Business name generator where you enter any word you'd like your business name to include and let it generate names.

You can then look through the list of proposed business names from which you can select your favorite store name. This will save you time, and it's free to use. But this is not a guarantee that you have a name yet; you must check if the name is available because the chances are that some names are already in use.

Create Your Shopify Account

Once you have a name for your dropshipping store, you can then go on to create a Shopify account. This is a quick and simple process. First, you'll visit the Shopify website homepage. While here, you'll see an empty field on the top area of the screen where you'll enter your email address and click on 'Get started.' This will prompt the next step where you'll be asked to create a password for your Shopify account as well as provide the name of your Shopify dropshipping store. This is followed by a couple of questions on your experience with e-commerce as well as other personal details. When you complete all these and submit, your Shopify account will be ready. The next thing you'll need to do is configure the settings of your account before launching your Shopify dropshipping account.

Optimize Your Shopify Account Settings

You'll have to go through the settings of the Shopify account you just created. This is important because it will ensure that you're able to receive money from your customers. It's also an opportunity to create policies for your store as well as establish the shipping rates.

Adding the Payment Information

The first thing you need to include in your Shopify dropshipping store is the payment option. This is a crucial step because failure to this means that you won't be able to receive money from your customers. When this happens, it means you can't do business. To include your payment information, go to the 'settings' page and click on the 'payments' tab. This gives you the option of adding your payment information. Generally, adding your PayPal account is ideal. If you don't have a PayPal account, you can simply signup for one in a matter of minutes. There are also other payment gateways you could consider.

Adding Store Policies

Before launching your own Shopify dropshipping store, you must make sure that you have the relevant store policies that govern how you will do business in place. Shopify has made it easy for entrepreneurs by creating a standardized refund policy, privacy policy, as well as terms and conditions for your store. You can access this tool by clicking on the settings menu and go to the 'checkout' tab. Scroll to the bottom so that you find the fields that are mentioned. All you have to do is click on generate, and you'll have your policies in place.

Shipping Rates

It's important that you clearly define the shipping rates for your Shopify dropshipping store. Generally, we recommend that you offer free shipping because it's the easiest option. Offering different shipping rates for different regions can be quite confusing. Therefore, make sure you incorporate the shipping fee in the price of the products you're selling and make the shipping free. For instance, if you intend to sell a T-shirt for $15, you can raise the price to $20 so that you cater for the shipping costs. Offering free shipping for your Shopify dropshipping store also doubles up as a marketing strategy that will enable you to sell your products. To set up free shipping for your store, go to the settings, and select the 'shipping' tab. Delete all the domestic shipping zones and instead add 'Free International Shipping' in the 'Rest of World' section. You will then select 'Rate: Free Shipping Rate,' and you have it in place.

Launching Your Shopify Dropshipping Store

Now that you've added all the important information to your Shopify dropshipping store, you now need to launch your store. To do this, you'll need to access the Shopify setting and then select the 'sales channels' option. Then select 'add an online store.' With these steps, you'll have your Shopify store up and running.

Designing Your Shopify Dropshipping Store

Although you have your dropshipping store ready, you're not ready to sell yet. You need to consider designing your e-commerce store because you need to present your store and brand in a manner that makes it stand out. Besides, you need an aesthetically pleasing dropshipping store just as you would with a brick and mortar store. Presentation is everything; it helps customers make either a good or bad first impression of your business. Keep in mind that first impressions can't be ignored because they count.

In terms of design, there are two main aspects you have to take into consideration in the designing of your Shopify dropshipping store—that is, the logo and the theme.

Selecting A Theme for Your Shopify Dropshipping Store

Shopify presents you with a built-in theme store that gives you access to a world of endless possibilities because you can source a wide variety of themes. There are both premium options and free theme options. Take a look around and choose a theme for your store. If you're tight on finances, you are better off starting with a free theme. Besides, since you're still getting to understand the Shopify interface, you can always upgrade to a premium theme over time. If anything, choosing a theme can be a tricky affair. You can look around to see which theme is suitable for your store before you even think about customizing it.

Creating A Logo

A logo serves as an identity badge for your business. It helps your customers to remember your brand with ease. Spend some time to figure out what you want your logo to look like and how you will integrate it into the rest of the design of your store. While the process of creating a logo seems time-consuming and tough, you can take advantage of free online logo makers to help you generate a logo in just a few minutes. You can experiment with the colors, fonts, positioning, and icons in order to develop a perfect logo that sets off your brand. You can also create a logo using graphic design software such as Canva and Photoshop. Better still, outsource logo design services from various freelance platforms at pocket-friendly prices. When you have the logo and theme figured out, your store will begin getting ready for business.

Add Your Products

When you have the store design ready, the next step is to begin adding products to start generating revenue.

Making Your First Sale

Now that you have everything in place, it's time to make your first sale and start generating revenue with your Shopify dropshipping store. You may not generate a huge volume of traffic just yet, so you'll do well to consider doing some marketing campaigns to draw potential customers to your store.

Optimizing Your Store for Selling

Traditional stores often use visual merchandising to help customers to find products they're interested in purchasing easily. For your dropshipping store, your product page will comprise brand copywriting, user experience, and product placement. When properly executed, these components will work together to generate excellent conversion rates for your very first sale. Here are some ideas you can include on your dropshipping store to increase conversion levels:

An Excellent Product Page

The challenge with dropshipping is that customers don't get the opportunity to touch or feel or even see the products before purchasing them. All they see is a photo of the product. Therefore, they'll judge the product based on how well the photo was captured. A great product page will generate great confidence that will, in turn, translate to higher conversion rates.

Product Description

Along with the product image, you need to have a clear description of the product that adds reality while also giving potential customers an even better impression of the product. This includes everything from the choice of colors and other features that make the product realistic while increasing the customer's desire to purchase. While you may want to have these in long paragraphs, you'll do well to consider bullets while infusing the description with your brand image to create a persona that is relatable to your customers.

A Clear Call to Action

You're getting customers to your page so that they can purchase the products you're selling. This means you must have a clear call to action that includes having the 'add to cart' option that invites customers to make a commitment and but your product. Your call to action should be simple, with no distractions or even clutter.

Branding Your Dropshipping Store

Branding allows you to build a distinct identity the eventually molds you as a leader or influencer in your niche. Eventually, your identity becomes an asset that you can take advantage of in advancing your business. Your brand brings in credibility for the identity of your business, thus enabling you to sell more products. In dropshipping, branding gives you more authority in your niche. Creating a perception of a flawless product goes a long way in a world where people value perfectionism more than anything else. Creating a brand requires you to be consistent in terms of quality and behavioral patterns. Two qualities that will distinguish you as a strong brand are:

Reliability

Money is not always the motivation. You need to make sure that you act in a manner that is deemed right at all times.

Customers will trust and embrace your brand if they are certain that you will maintain a good reputation as well as meet their expectations overwhelmingly.

Authenticity

A good brand will stand out from the rest even when the market is overcrowded. You can achieve this by being authentic in that you don't try to be someone else. This may involve offering something that other dropshippers are not offering because, after all, you can't guarantee authenticity in terms of the product because you're probably getting your products from the same suppliers as your competitors.

Conclusion

Thank you for making it through the end of *Dropshipping*! Let's hope it was informative has provided you with all the information you need to set up your first dropshipping store. The next step is to implement this and get on the path of financial freedom with the right tools. It's pretty easy to join the league of dropshippers and start making money from e-commerce. However, you should not mistake dropshipping for a get rich quick scheme—you must be ready to follow a certain path to execute your business well.

We have covered a great deal of what dropshipping is all about in this book. From the basic understanding of dropshipping to how to find the right nice and set up your Shopify dropshipping store, you have everything you need to make the next strategic move. Don't set out trying to be like someone else or simply settling for the generic feel; rather, you'll do well to infuse a bit of your personality into your store so that it's uniquely *you*. If anything, you have worked hard to identify the right niche, so it's only fair that your dropshipping store is a reflection of your brand so that you stand out.

Remember, there's no constant in dropshipping, so you have to constantly keep monitoring trends and your competitors in order to gain an edge. You also need to have the foresight and the right planning to pull through. While it may seem as though the bulk of the work ends with setting up your store, that's not the reality. You must work on optimizing your site before you can see the passive income begin to trickle in. Most importantly, work on improving your skills and knowledge to become a trailblazer, as opposed to trailing other dropshippers. Your dropshipping success will be determined by your grasp of this model of doing business and how it's constantly evolving. Therefore, focus on growth, great products, and customer satisfaction at all times.

Finally, if you found this book useful in any way, a review on Amazon is always appreciated.

www.ingramcontent.com/pod-product-compliance
Lightning Source LLC
Chambersburg PA
CBHW071407210526
45465CB00001B/296